"This is a fantastic b
by letting Jesus cha ........ about yourself and
others. As you read this book, you will encounter a riveting journey
of personal transformation. I had the privilege to witness Kristi's
transformation firsthand, and I stand in amazement. I not only
rejoice with Kristi in her victories but also in knowing that those
who take this journey with her will be led into victory as they
discover the power of letting the Word of God shape their deepest
thoughts and emotions. *Do not be conformed to this age, but be
transformed by the renewing of your mind*' (Rom. 12:2 CSB)."

**—Mack Roller,**
senior pastor, Glen Meadows Baptist Church

"With uncommon courage and transparency, Kristi Lasher
invites us along on her journey of self-discovery, self-disclosure,
and self-acceptance. *Naturally Curly* is a beautiful story of family
and faith. Kristi's story has the power to make one more accepting
and appreciative of their own story and their place of purpose in
the family of God."

**—Meredith Sheppard,**
First Lady of Destiny Christian Fellowship,
author of *Letters to Pastors' Wives*

Kristi Lasher
Rev. 12:11

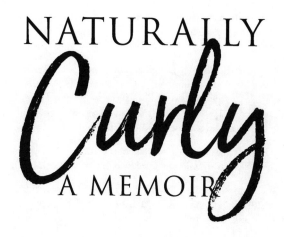

# NATURALLY Curly
## A MEMOIR

KRISTI SANDERS LASHER

LUCIDBOOKS

**Naturally Curly**
A Memoir

Published by Lucid Books in Houston, TX
www.lucidbookspublishing.com

This book is a memoir. It reflects the author's present recollections of experiences over time. Some names and characteristics have been changed or withheld to protect the privacy of individuals, some events have been compressed, and some dialogue has been recreated.

ISBN 978-1-63296-484-7 (paperback)
ISBN 978-1-63296-483-0 (ebook)

Special Sales: Most Lucid Books titles are available in special quantity discounts. Custom imprinting or excerpting can also be done to fit special needs. For standard bulk orders, go to www.lucidbooksbulk.com. For specialty press or large orders, contact Lucid Books at books@lucidbookspublishing.com.

# Table of Contents

# Special Thanks

To my King Jesus. You wrote the story of my life. You are worthy. Every place my foot has trod, You have redeemed. No matter where You take me, I am home with You. Do with it as You will. You've always shown up right on time— every time. I trust You. Thank You for Your faithfulness; Your unexpected, lavish blessings; my beautiful family; and for Your relentless love. You've healed me through my own story. It was worth every second, and I wouldn't have missed it for the world. I love You. You're always enough.

To my precious mother, who worked herself to the bone to provide for us. You were the most selfless woman I've ever known; you did everything you knew to do to give me the best life you could. God knew. He saw us. He knew you would not always be here with me, so He gave us Memaw who's still here with Papaw. They are still absolutely 100 percent the same, the most consistent people I know, and they are amazing. I could not have asked for a better upbringing.

Thank you, Mom, for loving everyone and proving that just because you're born into a certain mindset doesn't mean that it has to define who you are. Thank you for standing toe-to-toe with the enemy when you didn't have to. You bridged the gap. You refused to live a lie regardless of what the rest of the world said. You gave up your family and received a lot of persecution to give me life. Thank you for dismantling the lie that all "white people" are the same. That is one of the biggest lies from the pit of hell. Thank you for showing me how to stand out in a crowd and be brave and for giving me ancestors that will continue to empower me with purpose as long as I live.

This book is also dedicated to the family that I never knew—the family I dismissed. I am sorry. God disciplines those He loves, and in His great mercy, my ignorance and pride have been used for God's glory to create a new heart. I've been remade. I'll never again turn a blind eye to injustice, and I won't shut up about it as long as I live. My life was spared because of you. I'm proud to have been born into the line He chose for me:

> *From eternity to eternity the LORD's faithful love is toward those who fear him, and his righteousness toward the grandchildren of those who keep his covenant, who remember to observe his precepts.*
> —Ps. 103:17–18 CSB

To Jason, my favorite person in the world. Your strength and faith in the Lord amaze me every day. I've never known anyone like you. To go through the amount of suffering you do and remain a champion of the faith is indescribable. You truly set the example of what following Christ looks like. You set the bar for our family and encourage us to keep pressing forward in the midst of all the adversity that comes our way. I am so glad to be married to you and grateful that our children have you as their father. I couldn't have asked or imagined anything better. Your leadership secures us. We know we're safe and loved because of you. Mom would be so proud to know that you've carried on her tradition of spoiling me and continuing my weeklong birthday celebrations! I am looking forward to growing old with you and sharing many more years of this crazy, beautiful life.

To my three amazing children—Dixie, Maddie, and Jace. I'm so proud of y'all. I will always be proud of you. You are three absolute miracles who never cease to bring me joy. I love watching you grow; you are a daily reminder of God's faithfulness—each uniquely and wonderfully made. I could not have done this without your pure, untainted love. I love you.

Sunshine, you are very special to me. I know you've been through so much. You are tough like Mom, and you made me tough. Though we fought each other like crazy when we were younger, I knew I could always call on you to have my back. We had some rough years, but we also had some really good years and learned a lot. You took after Mom in so many ways. You have her looks, her laugh, her country twang when you choose, her drive, and her genuine heart of gold. I am so proud that you are my sister.

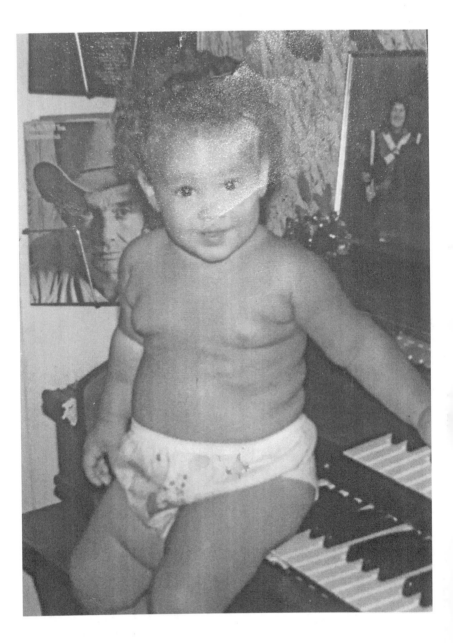

# Introduction

*He has made everything beautiful in its time.*

*—Eccles. 3:11*

As soon as I walked into my local Barnes & Noble one day, the Lord whispered, "Your book will be on these shelves." In this journey with the Lord, I have found myself chuckling under my breath in disbelief at the things the Spirit of God has revealed to me. On that day, I laughed out loud yet simultaneously became captivated by fear when I thought about Sarah and Abraham's story. As their story is told in Genesis, God promised Abraham descendants that would be too many to count. Despite his old age, Abraham believed God, and it was credited to him as righteousness. His wife, Sarah, had a different reaction to the news. She could not believe what she overheard in the conversation between her husband and three visitors:

> *Then one of them said, "I will surely return to you about this time next year, and Sarah your wife will*

*have a son." Now Sarah was listening at the entrance to the tent, which was behind him. Abraham and Sarah were already very old, and Sarah was past the age of childbearing. So Sarah laughed to herself as she thought, "After I am worn out and my lord is old, will I now have this pleasure?" Then the LORD said to Abraham, "Why did Sarah laugh and say, 'Will I really have a child, now that I am old?' Is anything too hard for the LORD? I will return to you at the appointed time next year, and Sarah will have a son."*

—Gen. 18:10–14

Indeed, at the appointed time, God did everything He had promised Sarah and Abraham. Within a year, she had given birth to their son, Isaac, making Sarah and Abraham the mother and father of a chosen nation. Abraham was one hundred years old. Sarah was ninety. (To read the full story, see Genesis 18, 21:2–5.)

In my deepest experiences with the Lord, I have learned that His Word is no joke, even as I have sometimes felt like my life was unreal. But seeing my life as a joke is completely contradictory to what I say I believe. It's crazy. I try daily to wrap my mind around the truth that God has entrusted me with this story. At times, I have been the absolute biggest idiot. I have showed out in the worst way and gone completely opposite the path I knew was right. But I couldn't sin big enough to make Him not enough. God cleans us up well, and He has great plans for us. Despite my shortcomings, He has been faithful to me and kept His word, even when I had no idea what keeping His word truly meant (though I claimed to understand).

Some of the events that follow seem impossible, events that I now realize have had healing powers beyond my comprehension.

If God was there back then, how is He not here now when things keep getting crazier? The fullness, wonder, and sovereignty of God leave me awestruck. His fingerprints are everywhere. His evidence is undeniable. He is incredible—invisible to our earthly eyes, yet indescribable. I owe Him everything. At nearly 40 years old, my eyes fail me, but I've never seen more clearly.

Although 2020 brought many distractions, I finally chose the better option. The Lord has set me free and confirmed His presence and promise, and He has opened a door no man can shut (Rev. 3:20). Truly, now I know what it means to be a vessel in the hands of a masterful Potter.

# Deep Waters

*When great floodwaters come, they will not reach him.*
*—Ps. 32:6 CSB*

When I was about three or four years old, my mother took me to a pool to swim and play. While she lounged by the pool talking to her friends, I sat by the edge of the pool hating the floaties that stuck to my skin. I had to wear them because I could not swim, and I remember my mom sternly telling me not to dare get in the pool without her unless I had on my floaties. But as I sat by the glistening water, the pool seemed to beg me to get in; the water looked so enticing, smooth, and innocent. First, I dipped my toe in, then my foot, and then my leg. Eventually, I pulled off my floaties. I do not know if my gradual testing of the waters convinced me to go full in or if I lost my hold and slipped in by accident. All I know is that suddenly I was submerged under water and drowning. The strong force of the water dragged me down, and I could not save myself no matter how hard I fought. In my own strength, I couldn't even get my head above water to gasp for air. Death would certainly have been my fate had I been left on my own.

Suddenly, my mom's hand reached into the water, and she grabbed me and pulled me out. Holding me tight in her arms, she hugged and kissed me over and over. She didn't reprimand or punish me for my actions—she was only thankful to have me safe. Little did I know this event would foreshadow a path I would often take as my life played out into adulthood. Mine has been a recurring journey of knowing better, refusing to listen, and testing the waters. Then I would find myself in over my head, with no way to fight my way out regardless of how hard I tried. Ultimately, someone would always step in to save my scrawny little tail though I swore I was bulletproof when I started down the steep hole. At some point I finally realized it was the hand of God that always pulled me out—no matter how deep the waters. And once I glimpsed the One who held me, I stopped and began to listen. When I did, I was assured that deep waters would continue to rise, but because of Him, they would never overtake me.

Nearly drowning is the earliest memory I have of my childhood, and it's just one of several near-death experiences I have had. When I was five years old, my sister was giving me a "pump" to the five and dime. *Pump* was '80s child terminology for when you sit on the handlebars of a bicycle someone else is riding. We were crossing a busy street when somebody wasn't looking, and a car hit us. It knocked me onto the road and knocked my sister onto the car's windshield. As I lay flat on the concrete, the ambulances, police, and bystanders began to crowd the scene. Out of the chaos appeared my mother, dressed to the nines in her '80s fashion: big puffy pink dress, panty hose, teased hair, and pumps. She was gorgeous. Frantically, she asked the paramedics whether we were okay. My sister was more banged up than I was, but neither one of us wanted to go to the hospital. We had nothing but scratches and a couple of bruises, so we loaded up the bike, got in the car, and headed home.

Another time, I was riding my bike through our apartment parking lot and got hit by a car. I remember being laid flat out on the hard concrete, with my only view being the car above me. Again, my mom ran out, pulled me off the street, and made sure I was okay. I was fine, just a little shaken up.

I also have a few memories from my childhood that I treasure. Each memory is truly a gift because when I was 16, I was in a terrible car accident that damaged a good portion of my memory. The wreck involved my car being wrapped around a tree, the jaws of life, a scary hospital stay with terrifying details I'd rather not describe, and several weeks at home completely helpless. I don't remember anything other than glimpses of close friends coming in and out to visit, and me requesting food from my mom but forgetting that I'd eaten only moments before. Memaw and Mom thought I was as good as dead. Nonetheless, here I am, over 20 years later, intact enough to relive the experience now as a mother of three. At the time, I thought I was invincible, and the accidents didn't make me "feel lucky" to be alive. But now I get it. I have a completely different, weightier perspective that makes me realize these incidents were nothing short of miracles—not only did I survive, but I was unharmed.

# Childlike Faith

*Jesus said, "Let the little children come to me, and do not hinder them, for the kingdom of heaven belongs to such as these."*

—*Matthew 19:14*

My sister and I were raised in a world where you had to fend for yourself. We had a single, hardworking mom and lived just a few short miles south of Dallas in Lancaster, Texas. Throughout our childhood, we were left on our own in many situations where we just had to make things work. We were raised to be tough, and we had a tough mother who contributed to our stubborn nature. My mom was a fireball who married a rodeo cowboy and then had my older sister when she was fifteen. She divorced the cowboy a short time later, deciding to move to California with her three-year-old daughter. My mom would create memories such as getting choked by security at a concert while trying to get to Elvis, going against her father's wishes by falling in love and marrying a Black man, and choosing to give birth to a biracial child in the '80s. She went against the grain, to say the least.

My mom was raised on a farm and loved to ride horses, letting her long brown hair flow as freely as her spirit. She was hard-headed, country, and as stubborn as they come. You couldn't tell her anything she didn't already know, and if you did catch her attention, she'd flash her proper southern smile, nod, and give you a "bless your heart" look to make you feel better.

My sister, Sunshine, is my half sister, and we look nothing alike. She has fair skin, blonde hair, and blue eyes. I had thick, black, unmanageable curly hair; brown eyes; and brown skin. Back then, the differences between us meant everything, though until I was 10 years old, I didn't know it. My sister and I were all we had some days, so we figured things out on our own. My mom would leave us on our own during the day while she went to work, and since we couldn't go anywhere, we'd play with other children in the neighborhood, scrounge up money by looking under the couch cushions and around the house, and order pizza with the change. Sometimes, we would sneak through a small hole in the fence that separated us from the Sonic behind our apartment to get ice cream with our leftover coins.

We also fought like cats and dogs. Sunshine is eight years older than I am, and she was meaner than a rattlesnake. She loved to torture me—I was a spoiled brat, and I'm sure she could not wait to break free of me. My mom would go out at night and leave my sister to take care of me, but since my sister hated having to watch me instead of going out with her friends, she would sneak out and drag me along. One night we snuck out to the movies on the square, but somehow Memaw found out about it. Suddenly, Sunshine felt someone tapping her on the shoulder and turned around to find Memaw glaring at her—a terrifying sight!

Our mom used to make my sister take me with her any time she went somewhere with her friends. Looking back, I realize that Sunshine had more than just me to fight with. In the part of the world where we live, she had to be strong. I remember her getting into trouble countless times with girls who didn't like her. One night as were leaving the movie theater, Sunshine's friends had to hold me back to keep me from jumping into a fight with a group of girls who jumped her as we came out of the theater. Another time, I vaguely remember standing on the second-story patio of our apartment, watching my mom hold my sister back from answering the taunts of another group of girls who were after her. Honestly, I was too young to understand the animosity between Sunshine and those girls, but I do know it was always over a boy, and the fights were always with Black girls. My sister was white. Not a big deal to an eight-year-old, but now I wonder what fueled the hate.

One thing was certain, whether my mom was cursing at a bunch of teenage girls in defense of my sister or at the Dallas Cowboys, on Sunday we were always in church. My mom grew up going to a Pentecostal church; she played the piano, knew the Lord early in life, and knew where her kids needed to be on Sunday mornings. We may have lived like hellions during the week, but at church on Sundays, we showed up like we had it all together. No matter what the week held, we were in our best dresses, and church was always about image. I sang in the choir from a very young age and grew up hearing the stories about Jesus and other men in the Bible who fought giants and survived in the belly of a fish. I learned how He loved the little children—red, yellow, black, and white—who were all precious in his sight. I wholeheartedly believed every word I heard. I loved going to church and Sunday school as a child. We got to eat pimento cheese sandwiches after church, and when you sat with Ms. Honeycutt, she'd let you have as many peppermints as you wanted during Sunday service. Life was perfect.

By the time I accepted an invitation to follow Jesus, I understood enough to know I wanted Him. At eight years old, I walked the aisle in a tiny Baptist church one hot summer day in the sweet little Texas town I loved dearly, to accept the Lord Jesus Christ as my Savior. The invitation was given by my pastor, and in childlike faith, I accepted. Some people can't clearly recall their experiences with salvation when they were children or realize that they said a prayer out of expectations. This was not true for me. I will never forget the walk down that aisle. I vividly remember the layout of the church, the pastor who waited at the other end of the aisle, the pew where I sat, the momentary pause as my feet hit the red carpet, the tug at my heart, and most importantly the force I felt as I floated down the aisle to give my life to Jesus. I was nervous, and it took a minute for me to step out, but as soon as I did, I felt as if I were carried the rest of the way. Although I may have had near-death experiences, I have never felt the power of a force that engulfed me like that. It was a strong hand that led me to the feet of Jesus.

When I made it to the end of the aisle where the preacher stood, we prayed, and I received Jesus. My desire was to be baptized. I wanted it so bad, but in Southern Baptist style, you were required to correctly answer a series of questions before you could be baptized. I remember talking on the phone with my pastor and answering his questions to confirm my understanding. This assures the church leadership that you are indeed ready, and it affirms your heart change. I was overjoyed, and at the close of our conversation when he said good-bye, I yelled, "I love you!" I was extremely embarrassed and remember thinking, "Why did I say that? Where in the world did that come from?" Now I know. The Lord was surely working in my heart from very early in my childhood. However, it would only be two summers later that my newfound first love would take a back seat as I found myself giving my heart elsewhere.

My memaw lived in the same town and, while my mom worked, I spent most of my time with Memaw. She was no blood relation to me, but I would never have known it. She met my mom in the 1980s when Mom was pregnant with me and working at Sears in downtown Dallas. When my dad left, Mom had no way to provide for us and once I was born, she struggled to keep up. At one point, I had been wearing the same diaper for days, and there was no food in the house. What's more, my mom had just been diagnosed with diabetes and was extremely sick. She came to work one day in that condition, and one of her friends went to Memaw and told her how sick my mom was and that she needed help. Knowing my mom's strong will and opposition to handouts, Memaw was the go-to person for this conversation. She approached my mom and boldly asked, "Sherry, what's going on?"

As Memaw tells it, my mom was not happy to be confronted, but Memaw made her spill the beans. Mom finally told her that my dad had left and that she was struggling to keep herself well and take care of us. This was all that needed to be said. That night my memaw, papaw, and another good friend they worked with showed up at our apartment, which was a disaster. When someone asked, "What are we going to do with all this stuff?" Papaw surveyed the area, looked out the window, and replied, "There's a dumpster." They didn't give my mom a chance to say no but instead worked for hours. They cleaned out our dirty apartment, threw everything away, took us home with them, cleaned us up, and fed us. And the rest is history. I never went without a thing after that day. Memaw was always my memaw, and I grew up with the understanding that this was the way things had always been. She was the one who would take me to school, pick me up, and have a snack waiting in the car. She dressed me and bought my clothes, fixed my hair, and made sure I had everything I needed for school. According to Memaw, I was hers, and she took it upon herself to raise me. She recently shared with me that people would tentatively ask her about me: "Is she Black?" Memaw would answer, "Yes, and she's mine!" In other words, back off. You didn't mess with Memaw, and people knew that. A couple years after rescuing me, my mom, and my sister, Memaw retired from Sears after 28 years and stayed home to take care of me.

Memaw grew up the oldest of six siblings and the daughter of two beloved parents, whom I called Nanny and Paps. But she lived in a world that did not fully accept her relationship with me and my mom. Regardless, she not only took us in, but she fought off a lot of opposition and stood up for what she believed. She lived out her convictions and gained the acceptance of close friends and family who ended up loving my mother and me the same way she did. I never

From top left: My mom, Sunshine, Nanny, Memaw
From bottom left: Dana (Memaw and Papaw's daughter), me

felt different. Her family wrapped their arms
the large, close-knit family I had never had. Cl
consisted of large gatherings, with everyone
the organ that sat in Memaw's dining room. Ev
Christmas carols while dinner simmered on the sv
of fresh baked rolls, pies, turkey, and ham filled the ʊɪr. After dinner,
gifts were passed out, and the room was filled with love, laughter,
and a thousand conversations all happening at the same time.

My memaw was such an amazing, strong woman. As a child,
the only time I saw her cry was when her favorite country singer,
Conway Twitty, died. She cried not just for a day but for a week.
Papaw resembled Conway in his early years, a freakish resem-
blance. Memaw fixed everyone's hair in the house and made up
my papaw to look just like Conway. Just like my mom's, Memaw's
personality was large, and she managed her home and everyone
in it perfectly. It was a refuge. Life was good and consistent, like
living in a typical 1950s household—you understood that you did
things her way, and everybody was happier for it.

Dinner was at six o'clock every night, no exceptions. People
knew not to even call the house during that time. If the telephone
rang, it was an emergency. Papaw would come in from the store,
put his guitar and things down, come to the table, and we'd start
pouring the sweet tea. After dinner, the women would split the
dish washing duties. She had a dishwasher, but it would have been
blasphemy to use it. Papaw would go sit in his chair or get ready
for an opry if it was a weekend. Papaw eventually left his job at
Sears and followed his heart's desires to open a music store. The
store is the only place I remember Papaw working. He was also the
leader of a country music band called the Shamrocks. He would
hold band practices in the small building behind their house,
which we called the music room. I used to love to go out there and

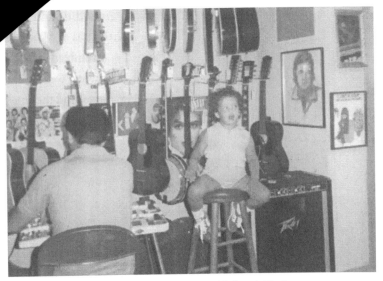

Papaw working on an instrument while I was in his store.

listen to them practice. The walls were covered in brown paneling and held autographed pictures of famous country singers whose songs he loved to sing.

They did a lot of business with country artists and knew a lot of them personally. I remember one night the house was filled with a little more commotion than normal. We were already in our nightgowns when someone rang the doorbell. After a lot of confusion, someone finally told me that it was Ricky Skaggs's guitar player, who had come to pick up guitar strings from Papaw. I was very young, but I wondered if I needed to go get fixed up in case he saw me. Memaw went to the same hair salon as Janie Fricke, another famous '80s country star we loved. Rumor had it, she lived in the same town as we did, so it was not rare for her to be seen on occasion.

Music was a huge part of my life. On Saturday night, if we weren't sitting in the living room watching the Grand Ole Opry in our nightgowns with a bowl of strawberry ice cream, we were at

Papaw sitting in his chair after dinner reading one of his books about country and western music

the local opry watching the next best thing: Papaw and the Shamrocks. My papaw's steel guitar player (my favorite instrument of all time) must have been named Johnny because all I remember is my memaw slapping her knee and yelling, "Turn that steel up, Johnny!" Music indoctrinated my life.

I always had Memaw. My only worry, if I had one, was the absence of my dad. One time my Girl Scout troop had a father-daughter dance, and Memaw made sure Papaw took me. She dressed me up fancy and added blue shadow to my eyelids, making a big deal about the evening. Papaw took me; we danced, and I never skipped a beat.

I heard bits and pieces about my cousins going to my grandpa's (my mom's dad) to spend the summers on his farm, but I never got to go. Memaw, Papaw, and Mom did a great job ensuring I felt loved, however, and I was not aware that hate prevented me from going to my grandpa's farm. My mom worked hard to provide for us, and she worked even harder to keep me shielded from a dark world I knew nothing about.

Some of my best memories were Memaw's neighborhood Halloween parties. The whole neighborhood would go all out to decorate, and the kids and their families would take turns visiting each house on the block. Memaw's favorite thing to do was make my aunt Dana dress up and sit on the porch to scare the kids who would come for candy. It never got old. Memaw would squeal and laugh every time a new trick-or-treater came to the door and was scared to death by the monster on the front porch. After trick-or-treating, we would come back to the house to enjoy Halloween treats and party with family and friends. I didn't know there was any other way of life. I was content.

My childhood memories consisted of porch swings, strawberry ice cream, catching crawdads in the creek, swimming in the summers, and knowing by heart every word to every single '80s country song on the radio. I had a great childhood. I loved my school, my friends, and my family. I had no way of anticipating the changes to come that would rock my perfect little world.

Memaw and me

# Leaving Home

*As far as the east is from the west, so far has he removed our transgressions from us.*

*—Psalm 103:12 CSB*

I t was the summer after my fourth-grade year when my mom announced that we would be moving from our home in Lancaster, Texas. She had concluded that our town wasn't safe for us anymore. The number of girls who disliked my sister was increasing, and they didn't dislike just her. Apparently, they and their families hated us too. Even though I was never told explicitly, I overheard that the more people moved in from Dallas, the worse it was going to get. Therefore, we would need to move farther south to escape the problems. Looking back, I can't say I really know for certain what meaning lay behind the word *Dallas* for the adults in my life. Dallas was a much larger city that came with increased crime rates and violence. Our town was growing quickly and looking different, and its new residents were compromising our way of life. We had seen our fair share of violence, and I can vaguely remember a couple of incidents from elementary school that would strike fear in a single mother. Riding our bikes all over town was not safe anymore, and there was a well-known "candy shop" in our apartments that lured children and sold anything but candy. I was about to go into middle school, which would have been an entirely different and potentially more dangerous atmosphere for a young child.

Our move devastated me, and regardless of all the things happening around me, I had no fear or awareness of division. I loved my diverse group of friends, and it's only as an adult looking back that I see that it was diverse. The families that were populating our town were Black families, and I had friends of every skin color.

I always believed that hate and fear moved our family. In reality, however, it was my mother's fears about crime and violence affecting her children that motivated her decisions, not hate. The only conversation I can remember us ever having about race happened much later when my mom commented about my older sister's dating life: "I don't care what color they (her boyfriends) are as long as they love the Lord!" Still, over the years I somehow formulated the idea that the people who populated our town were bad. I cannot trace where these ideas came from. No one ever sat me down and directly stated that one culture or another was responsible for all the danger lurking among us. At the same time, no one ever said it wasn't.

I have since heard how terrible my grandpa was to my mother after she married my dad and decided to have me. That was part of the reason Memaw and Papaw stepped in. I was not invited to join my cousins at Grandpa's farm, and we didn't have a relationship until I was a teenager, but no one ever talked to me about it. If they did, I don't remember, or I already had my mind made up that he was right to avoid me. I must have had some acknowledgment of the dynamics of our family. I do not know where my misconceptions about my worth began, but the events that would follow and the lack of conversation to clarify the ideas I was picking up along the way played a major role in shaping my vision. A divisive mentality became my norm, and the beginnings of a great lie began to form. It would create massive confusion and a chaotic mind as I navigated the waters of identity.

We moved only one town away, but the absence of everything I had ever known and loved made it seem like a million miles. I was heartbroken and devastated to leave all my friends, my memaw, and my world. I missed all that. But little did I know those were going to be the least of my worries in the months to come—ironically, our new town would be no escape for me. I would soon understand the hate I had known nothing about. Apparently, I was a part of the problem.

Red Oak, Texas, was ten miles south of my beloved childhood town, and the area was a different world 30 years ago. It was 1991 and I was at the beginning of my fifth-grade year. Nervous and excited for my first day, I walked into a gym crowded with unfamiliar faces. I recognized a few of my old friends from Lancaster, so it seemed my mom wasn't the only one who'd decided to move and maybe I wouldn't be so "new" after all. It was exciting at first to be in a different school, but as the days turned into weeks, I realized nothing about this place would be the same. I was heavily teased and couldn't make many new friends, and I slowly began to realize I was different. Everybody looked like my sister, and I was the only chubby, brown-skinned girl with an Afro. People were so confused at the sight of me, and I was so confused why they didn't like me. I wasn't Black, but I wasn't white. It wasn't long until I understood this difference was not welcome in my part of the world. I looked different from everybody else, but I hadn't known I looked different until they told me. They made fun of my hair, my skin, and my size. It turned out that I was Black and therefore disgusting. I had never known there was a difference between me and everybody else or that simply being me was wrong. I had been deeply loved and cared for by my close family members such as my mom, Memaw, and Papaw, but looking back, they were all white, and maybe I'd simply assumed I was just like them.

Two years after my conversion experience with Christ, I found myself confused and hurt. I didn't know there was an enemy and that he had plans for my life too. He definitely wasted no time getting started with those plans. I believed my classmates when they said I was disgusting, fat, and ugly—that I was not the right color and had the wrong hair. Unfortunately, unlike my near-death experiences, I wasn't immediately saved. No hand reached down, grabbed me, pulled me out of the mess, and brought me to a comforting place. No Memaw came to tell them who I was. This was not her town. I was extremely ashamed and never told anybody. It was me, alone, and I was on my own to figure things out.

By this time, my sister was already gone from the house, so I couldn't lean on her. My dad was MIA as always. So, I did what I knew: I fought. In my fight for position, I fought to be seen, accepted, and known. In my efforts for survival, I vowed to blend in. I was strategic. I realized each new problem as it surfaced and resolved at each occurrence to change what others didn't accept. I made up my mind in that year I would do whatever it took to not be made fun of or rejected. I would not allow any kind of difference between me and everyone else.

The most visible sign of my true identity—the one thing most bothersome to my new set of peers—was my hair. When someone offered to straighten my thick, curly mass, we got out the actual iron and went to town (this was the '90s, so there were no straightening irons). For years, I kept straightening my hair to get rid of what I thought of as awful curls that gave me away. I even started chemically straightening it at the age of 13. I did this every three months for 10 years. Apart from straightening my hair, I went without eating for an extended period of time to lose all my "baby fat." I changed the way I spoke and thought, what I laughed at, the way I dressed, what I liked and didn't like, and what I believed—all to be a part of something I thought was "it." I found a group of girls who I thought were everything I was supposed to be; they reminded me a lot of Memaw: strong, confident, and white. I idolized them. They kept me striving for what I felt I was supposed to be. I thought I had arrived. However, neither my peers nor I really forgot my true identity, so I continually stuffed it down and overlooked setbacks and sly comments, unwilling to allow what the other kids at school were saying to apply to me. I denied my reality like my life depended on it because at that time, I truly believed it did. I could not handle that reality, so I stayed focused on the new, "real" me, the skinnier, whiter version. As long as I kept up my appearances, I could win the battles.

I would work for many, many more years of my life trying to live up to that image. The day in 1991 when I walked into a sea of faces who saw my differences, was the day the great lie began to take root in my heart and mind. It would carry on for the next 26 years. I had said an enthusiastic yes to Jesus but would pledge my allegiance elsewhere only two years later. I quickly dropped Jesus and dove headfirst into a new image that I thought would give me everything I needed. I would soon find out that it would never be enough.

I still had to deal with insults and rejections, and high school only intensified my pain. I remember one time when leaving school in the afternoon, a group of high school boys started yelling, "Nigger!" while my friend and I were joining a line of cars to exit the parking lot to go home. She stopped the car, yelled something back that made them shut up, and we drove on and laughed it off the whole way home. I always laughed it off. I had to. I was too terrified of the truth. I took it all in, but left unexposed, it only hardened my heart. I still had a lot of good friends during high school, and made a lot of good memories, but I was too broken and sought the superficial to build up my worth instead of authentically giving anything in return.

During these years, I also saw fit to add boys to my list. I hoped that surely if I could get a boy to like me, I'd be okay. That backfired as well. It turned out that a boy did like me, but as soon as he found out I was half Black, he wouldn't talk to me. Word spreads quickly in high school, so I worked overtime to cover up for that setback and to create an acceptable image that would take me back out of the radar of ridicule. My skin got thicker. I prayed for it to get whiter and my hair straighter and less frizzy amid the humid Texas climate. No matter how much I prayed, the mental beatings kept coming, and no matter what I did, I would never be quite enough. No matter how straight my hair, those chemicals could never make me one of them. Everybody knew the truth about my identity, but denial was my forte.

Without realizing it, my heart slowly began to become callous, and I became mean, hateful, and awfully bitter. One time when I was around 15, my friends and I pulled up to a party and encountered an upperclassman sitting on the front porch of the house. When she saw me, she yelled, "Why is that nigger here?" The sting of rejection lying dormant from years prior finally flared up once and for all, and it pierced hard that time. In numbing the pain, I swore I would never again walk into another room unguarded. After that day, I was always prepared for a fight, whether it was another person out of line or a fight of my own in my warped mind. Merle Haggard lyrics became my doctrine. My heart grew more callous, my skin got even thicker, and I hid behind my walls built high with beer cans, my classic country music on repeat, and the "good-time party girl" mentality.

Usually, people I met assumed I was Hispanic, but where I grew up I couldn't get by with that assumption for very long. Everybody knew about the "half breed" who lived among them. I lived with a Hispanic identity as much as I could, though, and I learned how to use it to master an image that hid any natural part of me. My race was my biggest secret. It was my biggest fear. If somebody found out about it, I'd have to feel the pain again, and I swore I couldn't take that. I hid my real identity like my life depended on it, and at the time, it did. The people closest to me knew the truth, but I would laugh it off with them or remain silent to every racist remark, pretending it was no big deal.

Was I racist? In my core, no. But my silence would have testified differently. I never had thoughts or the heart to devalue a person, but I didn't have the guts to be completely honest. That was a fight I was not willing to have. I was convinced I was outnumbered. I wanted to be accepted, and I was raised in a system that I could manipulate to a certain extent, so I did. It was self-defense. I thought for so many years it was a blessing, to be able to lie and fit in. I perfected the lifestyle. It became so ingrained in me, just like the straight hairs on my head, that if someone mentioned my race, I became terrified and defensive. I had worked hard to get where I was, and the fewer people who knew about me, the better. I harbored so much anger and fear of being known, my entire manufactured life was driven by autopilot. By this point, I was well on my way out of Dallas and into a young adult life I could have never imagined.

# A Christian Attitude

*The boundary lines have fallen for me in pleasant places; indeed, I have a beautiful inheritance.*

—Psalm 16:6 CSB

During all of this, my mom never ceased to tell us all the right things to do, drag us to church, and remind us to "have a Christian attitude" in her high-pitched, southern drawl. I had no idea what this meant, and we never really talked about how I was dealing with my identity. I wouldn't accept the pain and rejection, and she didn't ask.

All the while, I authentically had a heart for God. I was heavily involved in my youth group. God had sent me some wonderful Christian friends, but I wasn't willing to fully accept them. I wanted to be the best, and for me a church girl was not on the list. My church and school friends were kept in separate parts of my heart. Church belonged at church, and school was school. There was no merging the two, and I would have been embarrassed if

27

they had come together. I was taught about my need for Jesus, and I believed I had Him, but that's where it stopped. Although I knew nothing of a relationship with Jesus, I had a great foundation in scripture and was surrounded by the love of the body of Christ. I am so thankful I had this community, but a lot of truth was left unstated and therefore a lot of questions were left unanswered. The Word did its job and created a holy fire in my bones that was lit within me, but then, my "real" life would put it out. My mind and heart were divided; I was trained well, but I was powerless and legalistic. In my next few years of adolescence and into my college years, I continued in my warped mentality, and because of my racial insecurity, I was not open to all that God offered. Instead, I navigated through life applying my own truths and ideas, which were intertwined with what I was willing to listen to at church.

Graduating from high school did not cure any of my insecurities. As I continued to vow to fit in, I transferred to the real world and brought my fake identity and anger with me. The combination of old hurts and the newfound freedom of being twenty-one produced a wild, reckless party girl who filled holes with substances that didn't sustain me even as I held on tight to Jesus as my sidekick. I had the wheel for quite some time, but thank God, He was a backseat driver. I lived it up as much as possible, wearing out the party scene in Dallas.

When a friend asked if I wanted to move with her to "go to school," I jumped at the chance for a new start in College Station, Texas. I went to college for a little while, holding down a job in one hand and a bottle in the other to make sure I didn't let my guard down. I hid my real self to perfection and continued to cover myself with relationships that agreed with my belief that my true identity was just a misfortune and better left unstated. Three short months into my college experience, I became pregnant. Since my significant other was never really accepting of who I was, a baby was not okay with him, and he strongly encouraged me to have an abortion. Being in a college town where these things were easily obtainable, I blindly agreed.

The night before my appointment, I tossed and turned and didn't sleep a wink. All those years in church with my self-appointed, warped mind, I lacked understanding and was unwilling to accept what God had for me. Thankfully, He never gave up on me. His Word, which had been sown into me whether I realized it or not, wouldn't let me sleep that night. The Word was doing what it was sent to do and was not going to return void. Finally, I called my mom early that morning and told her what I was planning to do. She said, "Kristi, this is all I'm going to say. They wanted me to have one with you." That was all she had to say. It was settled. She had never told me this before. No one who loved me ever said it. I had speculated, but now there was no denying why I was the only one of the cousins who did not get to go to Grandpa's farm in the summers: I was not good enough; I was uninvited and unwanted. That's why I had never met him as a child. I had never known that my mom had faced an issue when she decided to keep me or that she had endured hardship because of it. The only reason I was learning about it now was for the sake of her grandbaby. My mom instilled in me more than I could even understand at the time—an integrity that went beyond the value of hard work and determination. She raised two girls who would value life at any cost, and her unspoken example would lay a foundation for some of the hardest battles I'd soon be up against.

I hung up the phone and immediately called my unborn child's father and told him I would not have the abortion. He became furious and reiterated what I already believed, telling me how worthless I was, and then he hung up the phone. The Word finally combined with my stubborn will for good use, fashioning a decision that would save my daughter's life and mine. I canceled my abortion appointment, quit school, got a job, and started taking care of myself for my unborn child. I determined to do whatever it took to be a mom, and a good one at that. I had made my bed and would lie in it.

My perspective about my life completely changed. I wasn't instantly cured from my lack of self-worth, but I received a second wind to go on despite it. Even though I thought I was worthless, my daughter was worth it. She gave me purpose. I was willing to lose my life to prioritize hers. With this in mind, I knew I needed to go to church. I went regardless of my pregnant belly, which was visible for all to see. Alone in a college town, I got a lot of stares, and no one spoke to me. Regardless, I knew where I needed to be. I loved the Lord; I had just loved the world more. I had no way of knowing at the time, but a seed had been planted in my heart, and a process had begun that would move me to prepare for what God was doing behind the scenes. All I knew at the time was that I wanted my daughter to have the life I didn't have. Her birth brought me back to my need for Christ. I was still lost and in a lot of darkness, but the desires of my heart were beginning to change. I journaled my life away, mostly alone and pregnant in that college town. Those nine months trapped me with my unborn child, a Bible, a journal, and Jesus.

Her dad and I were on and off. He would come back around, apologize, pledge his life to me, leave again, and then repeat the cycle. Finally, right before it was time for her to enter the world, he was there. After his change of heart, our biggest disagreement was about her name. I had always loved the name Dixie since I was about six years old. Before I knew of a divided world and my position living south of the Mason-Dixon line,

I had seen the name on one of my favorite sitcoms as a child, *Designing Women*. I had no business watching that show, but something crazy happens between childhood and adulthood. As a child, I had an innocence that didn't catch the innuendos or recognize any derogatory terms. My favorite character was Julia Sugarbaker, who was played by Dixie Carter, and every time her name rolled by on the screen, I made plans to name my future daughter Dixie.

My heart had actually been set on the name Dixie Ruth. *Ruth* was after my mother, but my best friend talked me out of *Ruth* for fear that people would call her Baby Ruth from *The Goonies*. This made perfect sense to us, but my daughter's dad didn't like *Dixie* because he feared it would make him seem racist. This was the first time I had ever heard an idea like this, and I never would have thought of my child's name in this way.

In my mind, my child was going to be something new. She was going to do better than me and would live in a world that did not require her to fight ugly the way I had. I was very protective of her, and her name was part of that covering. I finally felt I had something that was mine, and I was not about to let anyone take that away from me. Dixie was everything I had loved and lost. Dixie was my childhood before the world crept in with its lies. Dixie had no color lines. Dixie watched *Designing Women* and heard no ugly words. To me, Dixie was a beautiful place with oprys, strawberry ice cream, lots of laughter, hugs from Papaw, porch swings, and guitars. Dixie was where the '80s country songs that defined my childhood all came true. If Memaw had her way, I would've named my baby Delta Dawn. Despite everyone's wishes, I went with my heart, and on February 9, 2004, Dixie was born.

As recent events have caused increased racial tension in our country, the word *Dixie* has become a hot topic because some people perceive there's a connection with the Confederacy. Some country music groups (e.g., Dolly Parton's Dixie Stampede and the Dixie Chicks) have changed their names out of concern that the term might be "glorifying the Confederacy."[1] For me, *Dixie* represents the South that I grew up in and loved and inherited—in no way do I use it to glorify any attempt to treat a people group inhumanely. My love of country music is evident from childhood, and I have the utmost respect for the artists who create it. However, I question the motives of these name changes. Hate comes from the inside. Name changes don't alter attitudes and beliefs. On the other hand, if the original intentions do not match the glorified suggestion, I'm not renaming—I'm redefining. Dixie saved my life.

# Enough

*Who shut up the sea behind doors when it burst forth
from the womb, when I made the clouds its garment
and wrapped it in thick darkness.*

*—Job 38:8-9*

Since I had a baby, I wanted to move back home with my mom in Dallas. However, Dixie's dad begged me to try to make it work with him where he lived. I initially decided to move in with him, but God would soon be radically altering my life with the most unexpected blessing in disguise. Before God made his undeniable debut, the devil had to throw in one last set of fiery darts. As a new, single mom, I was enamored with Dixie, and rightly so. She was all I could think about and handle, and I had no time for feelings of inferiority. I had to be strong for her. She would have a better life, and of that, I was certain.

Before I decided to live with her dad, we made a day trip to visit him. My focus was on my daughter, who was only a few weeks old, and as one thing led to another, the situation at his house became uncomfortable for me, and I did not want to be there anymore. As I started to load the car, a family member became very angry. Sticking their head inside my car window, they hissed, "You ain't nothing but a nigger, and your mom ain't nothing but a nigger lover."

It had been roughly 10 years since I had been caught off guard. The sting of rejection and humiliation jolted through my bones, and I kicked myself for forgetting my vow not to let that happen again. It must have had something to do with the newborn baby and my recovering hormones, but I gave myself no excuses. My radar immediately came back on as I reminded myself there was no mercy for someone like me, and as I left that day, I swore that my baby would never have to experience what I had to go through.

The pain was the worst part, and even though I held my head up high in the face of adversity, I was crushed on the inside. I became angrier, hung my head in defeat, and continued to believe that my worth came from the acceptance of people who cared nothing for me. I would still fight for it.

So, I stuffed my feelings inside, denied them, and reasoned that as a mother, it was my duty to do whatever it took to make things work for my child. I didn't want anything to do with Dixie's dad—his mom tried to make us get married because I was pregnant, but I refused. He begged me to come stay with him instead of moving from College Station back home to Dallas. That is the only reason I went back into the situation with his family even though I knew that they thought I was absolutely worthless. I thought if I moved back to his hometown and tried to make it work, Dixie wouldn't have to grow up without a father like I did. I thought things would be different for her. And so, despite my misgivings, I accepted her father's request.

Our living situation did not go well. He was abusive in all sorts of ways. One time, he got so mad at me that he dragged me down the hall, pushed me out to the porch, and reminded me that I had no family and there would be no one there to help me. So, I did nothing. I can't remember whether I slept in my car that night or he let me back in the house. He must have apologized because I stayed with him after that fight, and I continued to work and go to school. That summer I spent a couple of days away with my friends on a river trip in New Braunfels, Texas. When I came back, I found out that he had thrown parties all weekend, and then he called me one day and said we needed to talk. He told me he had found somebody new, and it wasn't going to work between us.

When I moved to Buffalo, Texas, one hundred miles away from my home in Dallas, I was still alone and unwanted. I felt I had tried everything possible. I did not feel guilty anymore, and I made plans to move back home. That is when his mother stepped in; she begged me not to leave and promised to help me in any way I needed. She also talked to people around town and found a place for me to stay. Since I was already taking classes at a junior college nearby, I decided I'd at least wait until the semester was over.

Apart from telling me to have a Christian attitude, another thing my mom had always told me was that a man would always let me down, so I should make sure to get a college education. I was in college through all of this. It was rough. One night, at my usual hiding place, my daughter's dad walked in. The man who had convinced me to move to that godforsaken town was with his new girlfriend. I was a regular by this time and had gained some allegiance, I thought, until I saw the bartender serving her drinks. This bartender knew my life story by this time, so I assumed she knew the girl was not only undeserving of her service, but also underaged. When I asked her about it, she said she didn't know and then kicked them out. A couple of hours later, I walked out to find a flat tire on my car. We fixed the tire that night, and the next day I was up and running my morning routine to school.

That afternoon when I was on my way to pick up my daughter from daycare, the drive didn't feel right, and I worried that something might still be wrong with my tire. After I called his mother, she told me to pull into an Ace Hardware close by before I picked up my daughter. What happened next taught me two things: (1) God doesn't forsake towns, and (2) you can't thwart God's plan, even in a Dixie Chicken T-shirt, blue jeans, and the stench of a backwoods bar from the night before.

When I pulled up to the tire shop, a guy came out to start putting on my new tires. I had to call my friend to tell her what was happening. He already had my car jacked up and had started fixing the tire. So, I asked him if I could grab my phone out of the back seat. Once I got the phone, I called my friend to tell her in the most dramatic way possible how I was being targeted and had almost died (not really) because of my flat tire. After my tires were fixed and I was backing out of the garage, the guy who had changed my tires mouthed, "Can I have your number?" Still on the phone, I asked my friend what she thought I should do. She was a hundred miles away, so it was easy for her to say, "Give it to him!" I did, and then I left to pick up Dixie from daycare and went home. Jason called me that night and we talked for a little bit. The next evening, he came over and changed the oil in my car. The next night he came over, made dinner, and then we watched a movie. Every night, he came over for something new, and we spent every single day together after that. Three weeks later, on March 11, 2005, we were married at the Justice of the Peace in Buffalo, Texas.

That was the day God said, "Enough." He was writing a new story. Hardships definitely weren't over, and some of the toughest battles I would ever fight were just beginning. I would find that going home to Dallas was out of the question, and I would fight the Lord over this and many other things in "the plan" for many more years. In not so many words, He'd reply:

> *Who shut up the sea behind doors when it burst forth from the womb, when I made the clouds its garment and wrapped it in thick darkness, when I fixed limits for it and set its doors and bars in place, when I said, "This far you may come and no farther."*
>
> —Job 38:8–11

# Stars at Night

*When I observe Your heavens, the work of Your fingers, the moon and the stars, which You set in place, what is man that You remember him, the son of man that You look after him?*

—*Ps. 8:3–4 HCSB*

The first year of our marriage was terrible. We lived in a couple of different places following his job in the oil field. It was chaos. Both of us had no examples of what a real marriage looked like; both were from broken pasts and fragmented families, and we were doomed to fail. We would soon discover that apart from the baggage we subconsciously carried, we were both also too stubborn to be the first one to bail out even though we hated each other's guts most of the time. We just duked it out instead—intensely. He still carried the mentality of the Marine Corps, which had been his life for quite some time before I met him. I, on the other hand, was completely undisciplined and accustomed to living in a house full of women who didn't follow rules and felt threatened by authoritative men. To say we had a long road ahead of us is an understatement.

In the first days of our marriage, Jason would jump out of bed at 5:30 a.m. and scare me half to death. I thought the house was on fire. Where I came from, if you got up at 5:30 a.m., you had better creep out of the bed as quietly and gently as possible. He was also in the oil field, which I found completely strange, and his work schedule was not normal. He would be gone for weeks at a time, living in a house full of other guys during those weeks. Then he would come home for a few days, and then repeat the cycle all over again. I was clueless about being a wife. I was selfish and really not interested in sharing my life with someone who didn't do things the way I thought was right. I longed for home.

We tried to move back to Dallas so my mom could help me while I was still in school, and he was commuting to his oil rig. This lasted for about three months until we realized that this arrangement was worse than before. So, we moved several hours away from Dallas and closer to his job. We were still miserable. The fighting got worse. I was full of pride, still held on to the unidentified anger of my past, and added new hurts and rejections by the day as arguments and words spilled over into my heart and attached themselves to my already broken-down mentality. I wished my marriage would stay afloat, but it proved to be another major life failure. I felt I could never be enough no matter what I tried.

Despite this, I couldn't give up because I was determined to give my child the life she was supposed to have with two parents. After doing everything I could in my own strength and watching matters just get worse, I knew exactly where to go. Back to church. Dixie and I would go to church as much as possible for several months. I do not remember anything I heard. I had a hunger for the things of Christ, but I didn't know what to call it. That same tug that had pulled me to the altar when I was eight years old tugged on me in these early years of young adult life. It would not let me go. I was making miserable choices along the way as the fighting was getting worse, and I swore somebody else was digging the hole I was begging God to get me out of. But God's Word was stronger than I was. It was beckoning and calling me. If I had only understood how fully known and seen we were, but I had no clue. After months of this, Jason's job situation required another move I was not happy about. However, with this job came the promise of a house near a church just like the one I had grown up in. I was hooked and ready.

In January 2006, we finally settled into our new little home. I was still 90 miles from what I knew as home, and Jason's new job required him to be gone for longer periods of time, but also home for longer periods of time. Our roughest patches seemed to be smoothing out, and I was beginning to get used to the schedule and new routine, though our marriage still suffered deeply. I loved the First Baptist church near our new house. It felt like home to me and made me feel I had some normalcy back in my life. We attended this church for some time, but all the while the tension between Jason and me grew, and it was becoming obvious that something wasn't right. I went to the pastor to seek help, and he connected me with some ladies in the church. We built a unique relationship, and they guided me with prayer through the issues we faced, beginning to talk to me gently about what it was to be a wife. Things remained rocky with Jason and me, but these new relationships from the church filled me with a joy and peace that had not been there before. All the while, Jason spent much of his time out of town working.

One Wednesday afternoon, I was waiting for him to come home when the phone rang. It was Jason calling to tell me he was coming home to get his stuff and then leaving. Confused, I asked why. After much prodding and trying to make sense of what was happening, I insisted he give me a reason. He wouldn't budge. It was then that I asked, "You cheated on me, didn't you?" "Yes." That was all he would say. A short time later, he arrived at home and as he packed his bags, I begged him to stop. I pleaded with him to talk to me, so we could work it out. Nothing I said made a difference. Instead, he did just as he had said; he gathered his things and left.

Divorce was not an option for me, and one of my worst fears was coming to life. In my desperation, I called one of his family members who was a youth pastor at the church that Dixie and I had visited previously. Jason and I had barely known each other at that point, and I thought his family, especially ones involved in ministry, could give me insight and hope in the situation. Unfortunately, this was not the case, and I received my first dose of disappointment from the church. I was pretty much told that regardless of what Jason had done, they would stand by the family and actually would prefer that I didn't contact them.

For a moment it became so real to me that I had never been wanted. I had tried so hard my whole life, but regardless of how I looked—Black, white, or skinny—and no matter my hair, straight or not, it would never be enough. I felt completely helpless; I was officially at my rock bottom. After I put my daughter to bed, I went outside, where I sat six months pregnant with our son. I looked up into the enormous sky that spread out over a ranch next to our house, and I demanded an answer from God. I was so angry, and I cried out, "God, I told You I would never get a divorce! What are You doing?"

I knew God completely understood my heart and desires for my life and my children. I knew He was in charge of all things. He had heard my requests, and therefore I blamed Him. I knew the One who had named and placed every star in that sky. I was certain we had an understanding. I knew this for sure because when I was a young girl in fifth grade, silently being tormented in my new town, I did have one friend. She was my first friend and was not like all the other girls. She never saw a difference in me. We became good friends for a short time at school, and she invited me to church with her. We would attend that church together for many more years. Even in the midst of all the things I went through in my youth, I had that church. My mom started going with me, and we were very much a part of that body of believers.

While I was in seventh grade, I was sitting in a Sunday service that seemed to drag on and on. As was my normal routine when sermons got too boring, I wrote notes to my friends. Since all the youth sat together during service, it was easy to communicate by passing notes down the aisle. One Sunday, I was so exhausted and bored to tears that I decided I needed to write to God. In that note, I requested three things for my adult future.

First, I was adamant about the type of house I would live in. In the part of Dallas where I lived, tornadoes were frequent, and I had recently lived through one of the biggest storms that had ripped through that town in years. It demolished most of the town, including the house I had begged my mom to stay in a couple of years prior before leaving Lancaster. I remember this vividly because we would go stay with my great-grandma on Sunday and Monday nights at her farmhouse in Lancaster. This might have been where my love of murder mysteries started because we had to watch *Murder She Wrote* every time we were there. But that night, a tornado warning interrupted our normal programming.

In that part of the country, when you experience storms of this magnitude, or if there's even a threat, the weatherman would advise you to take shelter. He would always say, "If you live in a mobile home, get out." I will never forget the sound of what seemed like a freight train right outside her door as we hunkered down in her middle room. My great-grandma explained that this was what a tornado sounded like. As a child, that equated to living in a mobile home and being outside while that freight train rolled by. After that experience, I became terrified of living through a tornado in a mobile home.

Second, I specifically requested that I never wanted to own a minivan. In my seventh-grade superficial mind, I believed that it would have totally ruined my life. Last, and most important, I begged God, "Please, please, please, God, don't make me marry a preacher. My life will be so boring." Not only was I bored to tears every Sunday from 11 a.m. to 12 p.m., but from where I sat, I could see the sweet pastor's wife sitting alone down in the front row listening to her husband. I thought, bless her heart, she has to sit there every Sunday for the rest of her life, alone, being bored to tears. "Please, God, no. I can't do that for the rest of my life!" There were a lot of other things that did not get written down that day but growing up in a single-parent home, I not only longed for a new skin color, but I longed for a daddy. I truly grew up with the notion that God and I had a major understanding of my "I would nevers."

So, there I sat, in a cold carport covered with a blanket of stars, recalling our conversation from my 12-year-old mind. No matter how ridiculous my theology still was, I was greeted with the warmest welcome. For the first time ever, I heard the voice of the Lord. He spoke to me. This is so hard to explain, but it wasn't a thunderous voice from heaven like we'd expect. I heard it with my heart. It's an understanding you suddenly have that doesn't fit into any category you could conjure up this side of heaven. It is not controversial, right or wrong. It is perfect. When God speaks, it's quick, poignant, piercing but gentle, firm, true, convicting, addicting, and the sweetest thing you will ever "hear." This is what I received with a smile: "*Well, hello there. Haven't heard from you in a while. Welcome back.*" The God of the universe had just changed the trajectory of my life in a whisper. If somebody were plotting my story, this would be the climax. From that moment, everything changed. The prodigal was back in the Father's loving arms. The next day I called the ladies who had been walking with me through the toughest parts of our marriage. They came over and comforted me. I was in no position to do anything—I was still far from home, alone with a two-year-old and pregnant. I had no job or any way to pay bills, so we prayed, and I waited.

That very next Sunday at church, the pastor preached on forgiveness. I have no idea what he said—all I remember is sitting there wrestling with God. As the saga of my dialogue with the Lord continued, I thought, "*Surely, God, You're not asking me to forgive him? It's been four days. I am the one who is alone and pregnant with a toddler; I have no job, and I'm an hour and a half away from home.*" We wrestled throughout the entire church service.

Ultimately, He won: "*For if you forgive other people when they sin against you, your heavenly Father will also forgive you. But if you do not forgive others their sins, your Father will not forgive your sins*" (Matt. 6:14–15). When I got home from church that day, I immediately called Jason, who was staying at his dad's house. I said, "I forgive you." He laughed and hung up. "Okay, Lord. Check. What's next?" By this point, I had fought so long and so hard in my own strength I was exhausted. I knew God's way was the only way. It was not going to be worth the fight this time if I did not obey every word the Lord spoke to me, so I blindly obeyed. I did not understand most of what I was doing, but I was done with pain being painful. I would rely on God to make it purposeful.

It wasn't long after that before God used the women from the church. They moved my daughter and me into a house owned by the church, with the rent free and groceries free. Affectionately known as the Harmon House, this became our temporary home. I was provided for in every way. I had no car, so they took me anywhere we needed to go. We were clothed and fed, spiritually and physically, and they walked with me the whole way. I knew absolutely no one, except a pastor and a couple of ladies from First Baptist Church. I was lost in more ways than one, in an unfamiliar place, but the craziest thing is, I was fully known and seen the whole time. God knew exactly where I was and who I was with. The One chasing me down was positioning me perfectly for a divine meeting.

I would soon be learning that God had some "I would nevers," too. He would never leave me or forsake me (Joshua 1:5). These were the days that our relationship began—I had the Lord all to myself, and I could ask him anything. This time was like a six-week-long slumber party with the Lord and a huge game of truth or dare. The only difference was that He played a little differently. Of course, being the gentleman He is, He would go first. I could ask Him anything, and I wanted nothing but truth. Sometimes, I'd have to dig for it, and sometimes he'd just hand it to me. He'd give me the truth, and I was dared to believe him. I inquired of the Lord about what He said about divorce. In my search, I found that God said He hated it (Mal. 2:16). Me, too. In return, the Lord would also ask me questions that He already knew the answers to. The questions weren't for his knowledge; they were for mine. His truth revealed the areas of my heart that were divided and why my best intentions and efforts were to no avail. I learned that in all my searching, He was all I ever needed. In a way that only God can, He made sure I knew that although Jason could be labeled the culprit by the world's standards, he wasn't the source of all the problems, and I wasn't the best wife, either. He made no apologies with this truth, for which I am forever grateful. With the help of the church and taking God at His word, I learned that if I wanted to get anywhere, I'd have to abide in Him. He told me things about myself nobody could have known—secret things of my heart so real to me it made the hairs on the back of my neck stand up.

I began to trust God and handed Jason over to him. I fell so in love with Him in that house that I ceased striving without realizing it. What transpired within those next six weeks is nearly indescribable. There was never any condemnation, but I definitely spent that time being confronted with truths that made me get honest. It was the sweetest and most bitter time of my life. I had no distractions. I had no TV, no computer, no car, and no family. Even if I had wanted to go out and drink my life away, which was my normal pain pill, I couldn't because I was pregnant and I had no car. No church ladies were going to bring me cigarettes; I wouldn't even have dared to ask.

Nights in that house were the worst. Nightmares came to life. I didn't sleep, and I was tormented by thoughts, visions, and un-imaginable scenarios. I had me, Dixie, and a Bible again. I would stay up all night reading my Bible, crying and praying. Until that point I had never understood anything I read in the Bible, but finally, after my friend switched out my King James for her more contemporary one, I could understand scripture for the first time. I remember being told that scripture was only understood through the Spirit's revelation, and I prayed fervently for that. Whatever it was, I wanted it.

Galatians 5:16–26 were the first verses that leaped off the page to me. On restless nights, I would work on memorizing that scripture, and within a few days I had it. I repeated it over and over. God became so real to me, and He taught me so much. He was my best friend and the only friend in that house all alone:

*So I say, walk by the Spirit, and you will not gratify the desires of the flesh. For the flesh desires what is contrary to the Spirit, and the Spirit what is contrary to the flesh. They are in conflict with each other, so that you are not to do whatever you want. But if you are led by the Spirit, you are not under the law. The acts of the flesh are obvious: sexual immorality, impurity and debauchery; idolatry and witchcraft; hatred, discord, jealousy, fits of rage, selfish ambition, dissensions, factions and envy; drunkenness, orgies, and the like. I warn you, as I did before, that those who live like this will not inherit the kingdom of God. But the fruit of the Spirit is love, joy, peace, forbearance, kindness, goodness, faithfulness, gentleness and self-control. Against such things there is no law. Those who belong to Christ Jesus have crucified the flesh with its passions and desires. Since we live by the Spirit, let us keep in step with the Spirit. Let us not become conceited, provoking and envying each other.*

The ladies from church came to check on me frequently. They were my first mentors and were so gentle and patient—something I was not accustomed to. As I grew in my understanding of my situation, God opened my eyes to my reality. With the help of my mentors, I understood I had biblical grounds for divorce, but the fight I was fighting was spiritual and could not be won by the weapons of this world (Eph. 6:10–17). Still, days turned into weeks, and I grew tired of the wait. I did not hear from Jason, and I really didn't feel the need for him anymore. I was at peace. I remember talking to him one time, but the conversation did not go well. Plus, I was so content with my situation having been made clean and was so madly in love with the Lord that I asked one of my mentors, "When are you going to take me to get a divorce?" This was probably about three weeks in. I didn't know it, but I was halfway through. I was told, "Just wait." In other words, running out and getting a divorce was not going to give me what I needed. Divorce would have qualified, in my case, for a weapon of this world in which the Lord was calling me to defy. All things were permissible, but not all things were beneficial. I felt as if God was giving me another directive to which I was well accustomed: fight. But this time I was to fight His way.

With every yes I gave to Jesus, my eyes were opened even more. I caught my first glimpse of a spiritual realm where things were more real than the things going on in the world that I could see. With this knowledge came great responsibility. I was entrusted with a battle that required that the book of law not depart from my mouth and that I was to carefully observe everything in it. I fought from the perspective of knowing who my real enemy was and the realization of how powerful my words were and how to properly use them.

My second and most powerful weapon was love, a truth I now understood because of the example so lovingly set for me. So, I obeyed God and spent my days and nights claiming God's Word with verses like Malachi 2:16, proclaiming His desires over my family. I was not only praying for my husband but also speaking against the enemy and his schemes over us. Then, I started loving Jason home.

This meant believing what God said about love. Love is patient, kind, and long-suffering among many other things, but most important, love keeps no records of wrongs. I had a lot of voices of people I loved dearly, not from the church, who with the best intentions, wanted to remind me of how wrong Jason was. But I had made up my mind to say yes to Jesus, and by doing so, I had to say no to the voices that contradicted His. I chose to quit talking to my mom and quite a few other well-meaning people until calamity had passed, and I stayed in the shelter of the Almighty. I could have done none of this without the support of the church. God's bride was present and being everything they were supposed to be. Without them, I would have been devoured by the enemy during this time. Even though my marriage was falling apart, God had a plan, and I believed Him. Sunday after Sunday as I sat in church, I would turn back to check the door. I just knew Jason was going to walk in. When the rest of the world thought I was a fool for staying and not finally taking my chance to go home, I had one voice telling me to wait, and it wasn't just my mentors. He had perfectly trapped me, and I am so thankful He had.

Nights were still messy. One night while I was fighting through a terrible nightmare, God said, "Let it be. Now what? What if the unthinkable happens?"

I answered, "You're still good, and You're still God. You'll still be who You say You are. I'll be fine." There's no peace like the peace that comes from the One who has overcome the world. My heart was finally postured toward Him in love because of who He was, not based on what He could do for me.

Another time in the middle of the night, as I prayed and cried out to the Lord in my despair, He spoke to my heart: "If I don't restore your marriage, am I enough for you?" By this time, I was so enthralled with Him, there was no doubt that He was enough. My answer was, "Yes!" A thousand times yes, and I meant it. I knew without a shadow of a doubt that God was on my side, and I was good with whatever He chose to do as long as I didn't have to do it without Him. As the psalmist penned, I could truly say:

> One thing have I asked of the LORD, that will I seek after: that I may dwell in the house of the LORD all the days of my life, to gaze upon the beauty of the LORD and to inquire in his temple.
>
> —Ps. 27:4 ESV

A couple of nights later with this declaration fresh on my heart, I finally slept well and dreamed I was talking to Jason. I woke up from that dream to the phone ringing. It was him. He said he was about to jump on an oil rig somewhere near Houston, and he wanted to first apologize for what he had done and let me know he would be there for his unborn son. He would send money for him. Jason didn't know where we had moved, and I didn't know whether he was on drugs or dangerous, so I did not want him to know where we lived. I told him to meet me at the church.

After spitting out a dip of snuff and putting out his cigarette on the pastor's windowsill, Jason walked into the pastor's office and about four hours later, he was on the floor, confessing, surrendering, and crying out to the Lord. Jason completely gave his life to the Lord that day. It seemed like it was out of nowhere—six weeks of hell, yes, but things I experienced in the Harmon House were amazing, and in just a blink of an eye it was all over. I have prayed for encounters like those again. It's indescribable. It's almost impossible to retell and do it justice. God is truly near to the brokenhearted.

# New Birth

*Pay no attention to things of old. Look, I am about to do something new; even now it is coming. Do you not see it?*

—*Isaiah 43:18–19 HCSB*

After that, our little family was on fire for the Lord. Our son was born two months later on July 6, 2006. I was putting all I had learned into practice and was still learning what it was to be home with my children and to be a wife. That little brown girl who had fought so hard to be a part of a white world was long gone and forgotten. Jason was working, and my mom finally left Dallas to move in with us, which was a miracle. God was so faithful to continue to take care of our family and provide for us. I had been so captivated by the Lord that I totally forgot about the rejected, nobody girl who'd felt unwanted her whole life. My attention had turned to my real enemy, and the fight was for my family. Jason was home and whole, and my focus was on this

FBC Fairfield, Baby Dedication Service: Jason and I with Dixie, Jace, and Maddie, December 2008. We dedicated all our babies to the Lord for the first time.

new life in Christ. Jason, apart from his marine mentality, had a drive that went a hundred miles an hour. If you wanted a job done, he was your man. Now with his passion for Christ, he took his work ethic and soldier mindset and lit it into a fire that burned ablaze for the kingdom of God.

He served the Lord in whatever capacity presented itself. He was doing street ministry in several different cities around the nation, going on mission trips, leading youth, and surrendering to any and every place God would have him go. We both knew he was called to proclaim the message of hope, freedom, and forgiveness to those who had been placed in his path. His voice was naturally loud, and it drew people—even more so in his spiritual calling. During an altar call in one of our first services at our large, conservative Southern Baptist church, Jason went up and lay out flat on his face. I had no idea what was going on. I went up to check on him because I had never seen anything like that before. It makes us laugh now because I was so clueless. With his full surrender to the Lord, Jason was radical and intriguing. He still is, but even more so. God took a naturally gifted personality and taught him how to use it for the Kingdom. It's still amazing to watch. His personality is magnetic; there is no better fit for Kingdom work than Jason.

Before the end of the year, he answered a call to ministry that would require a greater commitment from both of us. In a conversation following one of our date nights, I learned that the same voice I had heard under that carport overlooking a blanket of stars had also called Jason. The details of this call would again turn my little world, which was already rocking and rolling with the graciousness of Jesus, completely upside down. Jason was saying yes to pastoring a church. He would no longer be a street evangelist and then return to his normal job; he would be leading, protecting, and seeing people through the challenges that come with a life surrendered to the Lord. He was going to say yes to the God who had entrusted him with his bride. Both Jason and I were in for more than we could have ever anticipated. "Preacher's wife" was on my list of nevers that Jason, the Lord, and I were still very aware of. Apparently, I wasn't quite understanding enough of the God I served, despite my newfound knowledge of Him. Just like that night in the carport, I went to the Lord as the one being betrayed, and I reminded the Lord of our deal: "Lord, what are you doing? You know I said I'd never marry a preacher." As the Lord would have it, he reminded me that I hadn't married a preacher. Jason was the furthest thing from a preacher when I married him, and I still had a choice. He had kept His end of the bargain, and the question was whether I was going to keep mine. Jesus had just parted the Red Sea for me and raised the dead before my very eyes—how quickly I had already started forgetting. Even more than this, I had vowed to stay with Him, even if He hadn't chosen to perform those miracles. How could I leave now? Where would I go? Not in complete agreement, but blindly like clockwork, I followed. Where He'd go, I'd go, and as long as Jason was following Him, I was down for the challenge.

Once Jason started walking in his calling to pastor, I absolutely lost my mind. He would pastor for ten years before I came to my senses. In my mind, if he was a pastor, what was I? I had still never dealt with my identity. I had been so busy fighting for my marriage and family and navigating this new life in Christ that I felt caught me off guard. I became confused because a pastor of a whole church meant I had to do something. I still carried the fear of being seen, but I didn't know it. I felt extremely unqualified and scared to death. I had spent all that time learning who Jesus was, and I could believe He was who He said He was, but I couldn't believe I was who He said I was. Not with my background. That little brown girl suddenly reemerged and cowered in fear of a world that felt too big for me. I was ashamed because I honestly believed someone else could have done a better job, and I asked God to please bring Jason someone else. I was absolutely convinced deep down that I knew who I was and who I wasn't. Subconsciously, I still held on to the belief that my identity as a biracial woman disqualified me from any position that made me seen. I had no worth other than as my children's mother and Jason's wife. God loved outcasts like me, so that's why He had come to me. But that was it. It was just enough to be known and loved by God. In those days when I longed for Jason to walk through the church doors, I just wanted him to come and sit with his family, not stand in the pulpit. This was not the plan, and I would have a very hard time getting on board.

That same little girl who had made her mind up in the fifth grade to never be rejected again had been forgotten, but she wasn't gone. She resurfaced unknowingly and worked overtime now to keep up an image that I felt more than ever required perfection. Jason had no idea what I was fighting, and neither did I. Unbeknownst to me, the fear and shame of being known dictated my life and kept me in bondage to old lies I had forgotten about. In my mind, my race still silently equaled inferiority as the voices from both sides of my heritage secretly told me that races don't mix. These echoed in whispers on replay in my mind.

On the other hand, my husband thought my ethnic background was something to be celebrated. He thought my reluctance to accept this truth was absurd. My skin tone was one thing that attracted him to me in the first place. Anytime he would reveal my "secret," I would cringe, and I eventually let him know it was not acceptable and that it made me angry. Little did I know the explosion that was on the way.

# It Is Well

*The sun will no longer be your light by day, and the brightness of the moon will not shine on you; but the LORD will be your everlasting light, and your God will be your splendor. Your sun will no longer set, and your moon will not fade; for the LORD will be your everlasting light, and the days of your sorrow will be over.*

*—Isaiah 60:19-20 HCSB*

"Kristi, I am going to ask your mom to come live with us." I tried to talk Jason out of it. Even though God had radically changed his life, my mother still did not totally like him. He had asked her to move in with us many times before, but she was determined never to leave Dallas, and she never rejected his offer without an attitude. I was so nervous. He was sure, though, that it was what God had laid on his heart to do.

The next time we drove the hour and a half to see my mom, we discussed her moving in with us the whole way. I was learning to submit and trust his leading—which is really me trusting God—so it was quite the ordeal. She was in the hospital at Baylor in Dallas, and I remember him approaching her as she lay in her hospital bed. I thought, oh Lord, here we go. I just knew she was going to spout off a smart remark—and after all Jason and I had been through, she was not going to even pretend to be nice. She only tolerated him because of me, and I was terrified how she would respond. But to my surprise, she looked at him with those stubborn eyes and reluctantly said, "Yes, I know. God already told me." As sick and fragile as she was in that bed, she made it clear she was coming to stay with us only because the Lord had already told her first. The Lord showed out that day to me. It was a leap of faith and extremely terrifying to trust Jason, but God had given me another opportunity to believe Him, and ultimately He proved Himself, again. I learned that submission is key to God's design and that He could woo the toughest of hearts: my mother.

That year, she lived with us in Fairfield, Texas; she attended church with us and made a lot of friends like she always did. Everybody always loved her. They would help drive her to her doctor's appointments in Dallas while Jason and I worked. She and Dixie also spent every moment they could with each other.

I was student teaching at the elementary school, and early one morning the phone rang in the classroom. It was Jason. My mom had just come back from the hospital in Dallas the night before. He hadn't heard from her all morning, so he had gone to her apartment across the street from our house to check on her. When he got there, he found her unconscious. He immediately called the ambulance, and they rushed her to the hospital. For some reason, even though my mom went into numerous diabetic comas throughout my lifetime and always made it out alive, something in his phone call told me this was it. I rushed to the hospital in Waco, called family, and within only a few hours, we were watching her lie helpless on life support. The doctor said she had lost consciousness and suffered brain damage that would severely impair her if she did wake up. While she lay there, I read her favorite verses, and she would move every time I spoke. The doctors said it was just muscle spasms, but I didn't believe them. We waited the entire day and on into the night. Finally, Jason convinced me to go to a nearby hotel to get some sleep. I will never forget that night as we drove. I saw a huge blood-red moon for the first time in my life, and I remember the words of the Lord hitting my heart: "Take heart, I am coming back soon."

The next day, the doctors were pressuring me to make a decision. My mom always made a point my whole life to let me know that if she ever had to be on life support, she wanted to be taken off. She had reminded me so many times that when the doctors approached me with the news, I knew what to do. Of course, who do you think she had listed to make the decision? Her baby. The one who had slept in bed with her until the age of eight. The one who constantly ran into the back of her when she stopped because I was always following her around as a little girl. So, for the last time, I obeyed my mother. I told them to take her off life support. She lived for another twelve hours on her own. The only person I felt really knew me and loved me unconditionally left this earth on September 26, 2007.

Memaw cried at her casket. I'll never forget it. She said, "This is not right. Sherry, this is not right." It wasn't. My dad sneaked in at the back of the church. He didn't say a word to me. My grandpa, her dad, didn't even come. My mom was the baby. "No child should die before their parents," he'd say. She had lived her last

Mom holding me when I was a one-year-old

year of life with us. If it hadn't been for Jason's boldness, I would have missed that year we had with her. She was in love with Dixie, and Dixie was in love with her. God had provided for us when we had no way of knowing what was coming. Just as He knows now.

Even more, in a hospital stay only weeks prior to this event, my mom had expressed her love to Jason and told him she was grateful that I had him. As I think back on that, God also provided for her that year. He put her heart at peace. She was saying to Jason, "I can leave now because what God has done in you is authentic. I have seen it with my own eyes. I'm leaving my baby, but she's in good hands."

I went into a fog after I lost my mother. I do not remember a lot, but things started to go downhill. Our honeymoon period with the Lord was coming to an end. Life was starting to set in, and it was time to use all the truths we had been learning. I kept busy as a mom, graduated from college, became a teacher, dove into all kinds of Bible studies, led Bible studies at work, participated at church, and watched God turn lives around. We had our third child in 2008, and I eventually stopped working to stay at home with the babies as Jason navigated through his first position as a pastor. I had a strong desire to study the Word of God. I wanted to know more, so I enrolled at Dallas Baptist University.

I don't remember how I ended up on the worship leadership plan. I believe I thought I was always secretly supposed to be a country singer, and this would be my chance. It would be like getting a two-for-one deal because to me worship meant singing. The Lord definitely showed up and schooled me. I learned that worship wasn't just three hymns and a special by "sister so-and-so." Worship was the reason you were there. It was why you were singing. It was about the condition of your heart. Worship has many components. Preaching the Word is worship. The offering is worship. Gathering is worship. Prayer is worship. The Lord's Supper is a very big deal, and that's worship. I learned about spiritual disciplines, and the Lord answered so many more of those questions left unanswered as a child, questions I had even forgotten I'd asked. It was the sweetest time with the Lord. My eyes were opened, and I was on cloud nine. The DBU campus was full of biblical imagery, and the first time I pulled up to campus I immediately noticed a statue with Jesus holding a fishing net. Next to him was a huge stone engraved with the words "WILL YOU FOLLOW ME?" That question always burned a hole in my heart. I felt like God was directly asking me that question every time I saw it, and I was so excited to say yes. But I was quickly learning that with every mountain, there's a valley, and I'd be heading that way very soon.

# White as Snow

*Therefore let everyone who is faithful pray to You at a time that You may be found.*

—Psalm 32:6a HCSB

Once I officially became a "pastor's wife," it felt more imperative for me to hide my true identity. I thought if people knew the truth, my husband wouldn't have a job. To boot, we always pastored in small churches in the South that were in towns with a history of racism, so I assumed it would not be any different from the rest of my experience. I never gave anybody a chance. I was constantly on defense, and I didn't really want to be in that position anyway. I stood silent and passive as always on racist remarks, ignored sly comments, and passed as Hispanic when I could. No one knew me, so it was easier than ever to blend in.

These years, though, were so dark that I hardly remember anything other than the mental breakdown that started when a couple from our first church took us to dinner to "gently" break it to me that I was not quite up to par with my preacher wife duties. No one knew the silent battle raging within me, how I was constantly fighting to keep my head above water, and how all my old patterns were reforming and choking out the truths that had set me on this path in the first place. It was more than I could bear when I got the news that my rejection this time had nothing to do with race. My skin color wasn't even the issue this time, and still people claimed I wasn't good enough.

That dinner sent me down a dark hole, where I would stay stuck for quite some time. To cope, I'd stuff down the hurt, hold my head up, move on, deny a little more, and try a little harder. I had no idea who I was. Plus, I had lost my mother, and I was homesick. I started to doubt everything. I thought not only I was a mistake, but everything was a mistake. I thought Jason and I had married too soon, and he had taken me on a road I never wanted. It all became too much to contain, so I left my family. Not in a physical sense, but mentally. I found my moments of escape anywhere I could and was always looking for a way out. My soul was restless. I went back to my old ways. That same wild and reckless party girl resurfaced, and I was looking for love in all the wrong places. I turned my back on the Lord and started trying to gain approval anywhere I could find it. The most terrifying part was that if someone told me to be myself, it only created a bigger hole. I couldn't be myself because I hadn't ever known who that was before the dreaded title of "pastor's wife" ruined my life. I dreaded the mention of the title because I felt it imposed a lifestyle on me that I did not care to identify with, and deep down, I felt that I wasn't qualified for it. "Pastor's wife" was authentic, and I was artificial. I was already lost and confused about my identity as an individual, and on top of this, I was forced into a title in which I suddenly felt the whole world was looking at me, secretly defining me, which made me become even more fake than I was originally.

But I didn't know what I didn't know, and I couldn't be myself because I hadn't ever known who that was. It never once crossed my mind that denying the entirety of my ethnic background had anything to do with my faith. I thought it was still something to be ignored. I also believed that regardless of "what I was" God still loved me anyway, and He was really nice to give me a pastor as a husband and to give my kids a pastor dad. All the while I was showing up to church Sunday after Sunday playing a role, hoping I was doing whatever it was the pastor's wife was supposed to do. For me, the dreaded title of "pastor's wife" came with unrealistic expectations to be something I could never live up to.

That season of pastoring the first church ended very soon. I graduated from DBU with my master's degree and went back to teaching school. Jason left the first church he pastored, and we learned there was a lot more to ministry than what we understood. We were definitely called, but we had a lot to learn. We raised our babies and continued to walk—or, in my case, crawl—along with the Lord. Our successes and mistakes in our previous season of life had taught us a lot. A couple of years later, Jason was called to another church. I was not happy to have to leave my job again, and I was still not happy to be the wife of a pastor. I hadn't really straightened up my act, and I missed out on a lot because of my rebellion. I hadn't dealt with my mom's death, or anything else for that matter. Again, another small town with small minds, I assumed. Nothing different. I was gone a lot. Dallas was close enough, so I kept running back to my idols. Those same images I had worshipped early on were still my gods. I believed the same lie and I lived the same old story. I stuffed it down and made sure it appeared that everything was okay. I lied to myself and everyone else around me.

*But the LORD, who brought you up out of Egypt with mighty power and outstretched arm, is the one you must worship. . . . They would not listen, however, but persisted in their former practices. Even while these people were worshiping the LORD, they were serving their idols.*

—2 Kings 17:36, 40–41

The more I resisted, the more He persisted. My anger ran so deep, and my sin was so massive that I was convinced I had finally done enough to be officially unworthy, even to God—even to the One who had met me where I was when I didn't know I needed Him, even the One who loved the "outcasts." I had done it. God had pulled me up out of a mess and set my feet on solid ground, only for me to spit in His face. I was doing things I didn't know I was capable of doing and acting the way I felt deep down: worthless. All this while being the "pastor's wife." It was too much, and I eventually just became sick of myself. I knew better the whole time, but I couldn't seem to fight hard enough this time or claw my way out.

Finally, I just stopped. I had been trying so hard to get out of this life that I thought had been given to me by mistake, but God wouldn't let me go. How could God take a life that wasn't really even supposed to have been made and put it in a glass house on purpose? I didn't want to be seen. I was filthy, and I was wrong just by birth, not to mention the choices I had made on top of it. Not only was I stuck with nowhere to go, but nothing released me. This time, I was fighting against myself as His love relentlessly pursued me. As filthy as I was, He was there every time I'd turn around. I tried to push Him away. I just wanted to wallow like a fat pig in the mud. I was disgusting. But, just like the day I saw Jason for the first time in the tire shop, God was waiting for me. He knew where I'd been, but He had me covered.

I was completely defeated until I took a trip to Colorado. Lying in bed rehearsing my recent past, I contemplated what my punishment would be. I knew I deserved one. I had defiled myself, my marriage, and the life God had given me. My flesh was bearing much fruit. I knew He wouldn't let me get away with my sin. I knew His Word. I had heard it my whole life, and I had been a part of numerous, amazing Bible studies that had rocked my world. I had studied His Word in school by this point, and I had fallen in and out of love with Him so many times. I'd stayed up until early hours in the morning, reading, writing, and listening to Him speak to me and through me as I was challenged in my studies to seek His Truth and apply it to my life. I wrote papers, discovered truths, and declared my theology. I *knew* Him. But I had forgotten and chose to leave Him, again and again. I just couldn't, with the backdrop of my old life, believe I was who God said I was. I still didn't get it.

Regardless of my feelings of worthlessness, I knew feelings lied. Even if I couldn't fully ingest the truth, I made a decision to do what I'd believed. So, I took a deep breath and in my depression started confessing to the Lord. I confessed everything I knew to confess, still with the thought of punishment lingering in the back of my mind. I wondered when it was coming and what it was going to be. I also knew, thanks to my upbringing, that as much grace as God lavishes on us, He also doesn't let things go nonchalantly. I looked out the cabin window, not wanting to set my feet on the ground to face one more day. I was terrified of the unknown. This time, instead of a blanket of stars, a blanket of snow caught my eye, completely covering the ground. Instead of a cold carport, I was in a cabin, and out of nowhere, infallible words hit my heart: "White as snow." I was stunned. I knew that verse. Love had come to me again. This time it was deeper and wider than I could ever have imagined. In perfect timing I read that proclamation in *Fervent* by Priscilla Shirer: "So talk it up devil because as high as you choose to ratchet it up, you're only showing off the breadth and length of the love of Christ extended toward me."[2] Suddenly, another truth about which I had inquired of the Lord made perfect sense: "*There is no fear in love. But perfect love drives out fear, because fear has to do with punishment. The one who fears is not made perfect in love*" (1 John 4:18). Perfect love. There was no way I could grasp the magnitude of His love and forgiveness. He wasn't done with me yet:

> "*Come, let us discuss this,*" *says the* LORD, "*Though your sins are like scarlet, they will be as white as snow; though they are as red as crimson, they will be like wool. If you are willing and obedient, you will eat the good things of the land. But if you refuse and rebel, you shall be devoured by the sword.*" *For the mouth of the* LORD *has spoken.*
>
> —Isa. 1:18–20 HCSB

# Royal Wedding

*Therefore let us [with privilege] approach the throne of grace [that is, the throne of God's gracious favor] with confidence and without fear, so that we may receive mercy [for our failures] and find [His amazing] grace to help in time of need [an appropriate blessing, coming just at the right moment].*

—Hebrews 4:16 AMP

In the next small town where Jason accepted his second pastor position, I was still angry and not willing to give in to the pastor wife life. I wrestled with the Lord for quite some time. I didn't even know where I was—I had never heard of the town. It was tiny, consisting of two churches, a store, a post office, and our house. The first few years there were rough. For instance, on Mother's Day the two churches would get together and have a homecoming service. All the families would travel in to celebrate their moms or to visit the cemetery that sat across the street from our house. As the pastor's family, we were always in charge of something. One year, either my daughter or I were expected to sing, and my younger two children entertained in some way. Either way, I was in charge and scurrying around to make the necessary arrangements—all while I was missing my mom like crazy. It seemed that the farther God positioned us away from Dallas, the sadder I became.

I made myself go to the service because I had to. Every Mother's Day is hard, but that year, as I looked around at all the generations of mothers with their families, I thought, "God, really? Not only are You going to move me out in the middle of nowhere, doing a job I did not sign up for, but I have to sit here and be tortured by these families with their moms, moms, moms, moms? While I'm without one and a thousand miles from home? I don't even know where I am, and **You** took my mom away!" I let Him have it. Of course, as was customary, I blamed Him. It was all His fault, and it was all wrong. How could this be His plan?

In my frustration, the Lord replied with a message I'd never heard before. He said, "You left her first." His voice always calmed my storms. When I was in the Harmon House, I had a choice. I could have gone home, and I had biblical grounds for divorce. My mom hated Jason's guts and had begged me to come home. But the Lord was telling me to wait. I had said yes to Jesus, and no to my mother. What He said to me on that Mother's Day reminded me that I did sign up for this—I chose Him, and I left her. It wasn't harsh; it was the truth. After I finally calmed down, the Lord whispered, "Am I *still* enough?" He took me right back to the night before he brought Jason back. Everything faded, and it was just Him and me again. With a smile in my heart and tears in my eyes, I replied, "Yes, Lord. Of course, You are."

Jason and I in Colorado

I finally decided to get my act together and apply for some teaching jobs in my new area. I was hired to teach seventh-grade English. Teaching junior high opened my eyes as I watched children fight some of the same battles and believe some of the same lies I had when I was their age. The choices I'd made as a young girl—like trying to hide and fit in—were highlighted, and I began to be able to trace back some of the dark paths to their origin. Some of these kids encouraged me as they handled things much better than I would have, and as I watched others, I wanted to jump in and defend them from an ugly, lying world that they worked hard to be part of. God positioned me so perfectly with a new set of eyes that kept me on my knees for these kids and the choices they were making, but mostly He used it to show me areas of my dark heart that were still there. God was setting me up again, and He used a Bible study I was going through along with the situations I faced while teaching. I would soon discover hidden areas of my own heart that needed exposing—a discovery that would come through my being completely honest with Him. Of all the places the Lord and I had been through until that point, I heard something from Him that He had never addressed before. A lot of my dishonesty stemmed from my refusal to recognize my racial identity. It was not, in fact, a little deal that could be tossed to the side, overlooked and forgotten. It was a very big deal.

With honesty and sincerity at the forefront of my mind, I had to go talk to my boss about an issue I was having with a student. Our conversation about the student reached a place where in order for me to make my point, I had to be honest and share with her that I was biracial. I had never volunteered that information. Her reaction was typical: She was shocked, but surprisingly she commented that she thought I was Italian. That was definitely a first, and even though I was nervous, I had a supernatural confidence about confiding in her that day. I left her office not fully understanding what had just taken place, but I was certain the Lord had something to do with it.

The experience was liberating, but that weekend, fear fell back over me. Through a dream I had, I woke up thinking that it was to my benefit to keep my race to myself. That conversation with my boss would be the last time I volunteered that information, I reasoned. It is true that in the past it had helped some people because after they got to know me, it had broken down some walls when they realized the truth. They were able to see that race had nothing to do with the character of a person since they were able to get to know me first, without any prejudgments. I wanted to continue to be used to break down walls, in my own life and also in others, so I figured it was noble to continue to keep my secret.

But as the Lord would have it, I'd never have another chance to deny myself. Word had gotten out, and the next day my race was the topic of the lunch table. One of the teachers nonchalantly remarked, "I didn't know you were biracial." Immediately, my guard went up against old fears. I was terrified, my thoughts started racing, and I muttered a vague response. I had a full conversation in my head believing that all my relationships and whatever status I thought I had were gone. But then I told myself, "No, forget them. Let it expose ugly hearts. Let God use it for His glory." My Dad had ripped off my Band-Aid, and I panicked. I guess, He'd had enough. It was time to set a captive free. I tried to stay positive and told myself I was proud to do it for the glory of God, assuming all my friendships were over. That was when another teacher chimed in with a comment that would change my life forever. She said, "Oh, you look like Meghan Markle!" *Who?* I had never heard that name. She said, "You know, the actress, the princess . . . Prince Harry?" Blah, blah, blah. That was all I could hear at that point; I just wanted to crawl in a hole and die. I had no idea who she was talking about, so I said, "I'll have to look her up."

I trudged through my afternoon classes. As soon as school was over, I went straight home, got into bed, pulled the covers up to my neck, and lay in the dark replaying the day. Thinking about what the teacher had said, I got out my phone and googled "Meghan Markle." I learned she was about to become an American Princess, and I kept looking at her, searching and reading. I sat up in bed astonished at what I was reading. Her mother is Black, and her father is white. I was shocked. Her birthday, two days before mine, was the same year. It took a minute for all this to soak in. Although, I thought, my reality is Gause, Texas. Good for her. Still depressed, I lay back in bed and started flipping through channels on the TV. I landed on a special that had already begun on CBS. "Meghan Markle: The American Princess." Okay, God, I'm listening. I learned that she had experienced some of the same rejections I had. And even now, people didn't want "color" in the spotlight. Watching her confident and strong made me a little sad, and I wondered how on earth we had grown up at the same time but worlds apart. It also started to plant seeds of courage, and I began to be confident in who I was. I couldn't thank the Lord enough for opening my eyes, for exposing the truth, and for being faithful beyond anything I could ever imagine.

It was no coincidence that I began learning about Meghan roughly one month before the royal wedding. When I first heard of her, I was eating lunch with the same group of teachers I had eaten with all year long, but only God knew I had a secret. The secret I had, if exposed, had proved itself to do only damage. I had become a sworn enemy to a part of my identity, and that belief system ruined my life for years. As I grew up, this secret created division and separated me from the things I desired and the things I thought I was entitled to. If this secret was exposed, I was a goner among a new set of friends. At thirty-six years old, I sat as a professional adult terrified the day it was revealed. As one thing led to another, I realized that the ugly heart in the lunchroom that day belonged to me. I had no idea where I stood in my own identity. I began to ponder how someone's own mind could be so warped inside the very house made by the One she claimed to worship. The enemy had stolen so much from me, and thirty-six years later, I was a prisoner to my self-appointed, segregated mind. It wasn't the reaction of the other teachers that scared me that day, it was mine.

God used this occurrence to begin to unravel the truth about the damage being done in my life. I began to closely follow Meghan and Harry. Not only was Meghan biracial, but Harry had red hair. As if God didn't know, I told him, "Lord, Jason has red hair." Maybe it's a coincidence, or maybe God has a way of making a point. Things continued to get better. May 19, 2018, was

Harry and Meghan's wedding day. Since we had to travel out of town for my daughter's singing and piano lesson that morning, I recorded the wedding and was so excited to get home and watch it. I watched that wedding like my life depended on it. I watched the Lifetime movie, I listened to all the commentary during the ceremony, and I watched the famous "stars" file in. But what I still can't get over, amid all the pomp and circumstance, was the still, small voice that said, "You are that princess." Her strength, integrity, honor, courage, beauty, dignity, and confidence—all of these spoke loud and clear to me. I was watching the human version that encompassed everything God had tried to get through to me my whole life. Meghan had never let the voices stop her. She had kept going and continued to overcome. I could not help but lament the years I had lost because I believed the lies: my—entire—life. I had fallen into so many traps because of my insecurities. They imprisoned me. I would have to forgive those I harbored bitterness toward, and I'd have to forgive myself. I cannot describe the liberation I felt watching Meghan approach the throne with boldness and take her place among a royal family.

I felt like the Lord was saying, "See, I told you. Just like that, *this* is who you are." For such a time as this. I couldn't hold back my tears that day. *This* was the fairy tale. Not because of a royal wedding or a prince and a princess but because of the union Jesus was confirming. I finally understood the reality of how He saw me. He indeed loved me. He not only saw me, but He loved me. And I knew He loved me because He wasn't going to let me continue in the destructive life I was still subconsciously leading. I was His. Although I was dead, He was bringing my mortal body to life. I resolved that day that He would surely do it. Whatever it was He wanted to do with this life, He would do.

# Follow Me

*For whoever wants to save his life will lose it, but whoever loses his life because of me and the gospel will save it.*

—*Mark 8:35 CSB*

A few months after the lunch table experience, I found myself in another situation that caught me completely off guard. I was at a conference with my husband where most of the topics were on the racial concepts concerning the church—topics I had forgotten applied to me until the Lord showed up again. Out of the blue, a friend of ours commented, "I didn't know you had Black in you." My husband, three other pastors, and I were standing in a group, and just like the day at the lunch table, I became terrified and at a loss for words. I muttered that my race was not information I usually volunteered before my husband stepped in and explained how that was now in the process of changing. And yes, it was, but it was obviously still a deep-rooted issue whose existence I couldn't even explain. Still, the exposure was good, but I didn't know what I was supposed to do with it.

I had spent my entire life trying to lose any trace of Blackness, and fear set over me when someone would mention it. I just could not understand why. According to the content at the conference, I wasn't alone and there was much tension going on in the church over the topics surrounding race. I wanted to dismiss the idea that race was still an issue, especially in the church, and say we had moved on as a society. I subconsciously argued that racism was a thing of the past, especially since I was accepted that day at the lunch table when the other teachers learned my racial identity. I thought, I'm crazy. Nobody even cares anymore. Since my life had turned out well, I thought racism was over, but I could not escape what I had heard in these sessions and most importantly what God had already spoken to me in a whisper.

The conference speakers said Sundays were the most segregated time of the week, meaning that we all gathered on Sundays in the flesh but were divided in spirit. This separation is in total opposition to who He is and the purposes of His church. Obviously, being raised in the South, I was aware of Black churches and white churches, but what I never thought about was why they existed. These institutions were such a normal part of life to me that I never had any urge to think about them. It was a huge but somehow subliminal divisive mechanism hindering the body of Christ. If I were honest, at the time, I did not want people in my church to know my identity, so I guess I could relate. Mainly, it was the older crowd I avoided for fear of rejection; I had felt this tension during my entire experience as a pastor's wife, but I would have taken this feeling to my grave if God hadn't intervened.

I hadn't understood what caused me to think this way, and I certainly had no proof. I didn't know where the fear of revealing my true identity in the church was coming from. I didn't know whether this was due to the strain on relationships between my grandpa and my dad, or whether it was my experiences in high school that had a lasting impact, or a combination of both. I have no hard feelings toward any of the people in my past.

But I began to ponder my past experiences in light of what I was learning at the conference. Over the years, the relationship between my grandpa and mom was restored. There was forgiveness, and he eventually loved me and my sister's kids. We even lived with him when I was a teenager. He already had a relationship with my kids at the time of my mom's death. He loved Dixie, and Dixie loved him. But because I called my sister and she brought her Black boyfriend to the hospital to see my mom, he blamed both of us, and our relationship was strained again. My grandpa was a man of his word, and there wasn't much room for compromise in his beliefs. He believed that you worked hard and drove a Chevy, and he'd always say, if you don't work, you don't eat. For him, right was right and wrong was wrong, and there was no crossing the two.

Apparently I was supposed to know what I had done wrong, but I didn't. Someone had to explain the hospital offense to me later. Even though I knew my grandpa's hard heart, I saw past it. I cared more to honor my mother and fight for the relationship she held so dear. Reconciliation was important to her. We used to take my kids out to Grandpa's place often when she was alive, along with my sister's biracial kids. He loved them, too. People would sometimes say that he didn't know they were mixed, so he wouldn't be upset. We would simply go on as if that mentality were totally normal. He'd give the kids treats, take them to eat, or let them have a day at the farm exploring, riding tractors, and being pulled in a trailer behind a tractor or lawn mower. The kids loved being with him.

After the hospital incident, Grandpa would not talk to us or my kids. Dixie had just lost my mother, and I was not going to let her lose another grandparent. I decided to do whatever it took to restore the relationship. It took months and a lot of prayer to heal our relationship, but eventually our relationship was restored. We saw him as much as we could before we moved over two hours away to pastor a new church. Even then, we tried to stay in touch as much as possible and even took the kids to see him a couple of times when we first moved. But his health declined; the distance made it difficult; and with new jobs, church, and school, we drifted apart.

We called as much as we could, but when we did get to talk to him, he couldn't hear the kids. A lot of time went by, and we wondered how he was doing when we couldn't get hold of him. Finally, I found out from a family member that he had passed. They had the funeral for him, yet no one ever called us. It broke our hearts, and the news was a little rough on the kids, but we explained everything. We were all okay after some time, and they were left only with good memories. The connection was real. Grandpa knew. I knew. My husband and my kids, knew. Most importantly, God looks at a man's heart, and who knows if that time was not my grandpa's do-over? I didn't get to go to the farm as a child, but my kids did.

No one ever said anything racist to me at church, but I have wondered whether the relationships in my family have made me suspicious of everyone. I remained paranoid and defensive most of the time. All I knew was that some people did not like me because of my race, and I'd tried so hard to save myself but failed so miserably. I'd pursued various passions to fill the void, but all this pursuit did was lead me further into a pit of despair. The fear that struck in me each time I was confronted with my race told me it was time to take up my cross. Jesus said, *"If anyone wants to follow after me, let him deny himself, take up his cross, and follow me. For whoever wants to save his life will lose it, but whoever loses his life because of me and the gospel will save it"* (Mark 8:34–35 CSB).

Not much later, the Lord began to unravel some realities I had felt but couldn't explain. A man who had strongly disagreed with my husband about something at church confronted him one day. In his anger at my husband's not caving to his demands, the man made a disgusting racist remark about our church. When my husband originally shared this conversation with me, he did so much more politely, using "Black church" instead of the man's actual words, which I later learned were words I had been well acquainted with. Regardless of the milder vocabulary, it still punctured an old wound and shed light on the hostility that lay dormant beneath the surface. For the next couple of Sundays, I stayed on alert and waited eagerly for an opportunity to cross paths with this man to make sure he knew how "Black" our church really was. He had no idea about the identity of his pastor's wife, and I was determined to either make him angrier or feel really stupid. Both would have been great at the time. However, the Lord saved me from that disaster, as the man never showed up. So, I did like normal: stuffed it down, rolled my eyes in disgust, and chalked it up to the small-town ignorance I was accustomed to. I was so busy teaching school and raising a family that I forgot all about it, which was a blessing from God at the time. The time delay allowed my anger to calm, but the truth God was revealing to me was not over. It would be about a year or so later, once I was truly over the sting of the statement, that God would bring it back up. But before that, there was one more nudge of the Lord that would make His message completely clear and break my silence for good. *"Every kingdom divided against itself is headed for destruction, and a house divided against itself falls"* (Luke 11:17 CSB).

In March 2020, our spring break turned into an extension that would last until the new 2020–2021 school year. Our whole world turned upside down when COVID-19 hit our country. With time no longer an issue, I sought the Lord, and He revealed another area that needed attention in my life. As I had a break from my distractions, He reminded me there was something else I had never fully accepted. He placed a question on the table and gave me another choice to make.

"Truth or dare?"

"Truth."

"Are you ready to accept the position of pastor's wife?"

\* \* \*

This time, my answer didn't come so quickly. I had seen the toll ministry had taken on my husband. I knew now that life in ministry was anything but boring, and now with my deep root exposed, I was well on my way to curing any insecurities in who I was. There was no more room for excuses, so what was stopping me? Regarding the pain of ministry, the Lord assured me that people were going to let me down. It was a matter of whether I'd choose to do it with Him or without Him. Put that way, of course I would go with Him. Check. He won again. And so, the 12-year-old girl who begged God not to let her marry a preacher suddenly surrendered completely to the call of being a pastor's wife. That was just the beginning.

When I inquired of the Lord what next steps to take, I understood I needed to start where I was with what I had. For the first time, I reached out to the ladies of our congregation. We made efforts to stay connected and prayed together frequently during quarantine. We began a Bible study. I didn't know my calling would ever amount to anything other than those few things, but the end of May 2020 revealed a greater need within my midst that made God's voice clearer than ever. As I sat by the pool watching my kids play on Memorial Day when we celebrate those who gave their lives for us, my mind was troubled because I had just been made aware of a life that had been lost so foolishly. As I began to understand more about what was going on in our country, I started to realize what God was saying to me. I was disturbed by the situation, and my 16-year-old, sweet Dixie shared with me she had seen a video I refused to watch. When she told me that she had seen the video of George Floyd being murdered, I didn't even know what to say. I explained to her that I couldn't watch it. I knew I would lose my mind. Knowing about it was enough for me, and if she had asked me ahead of time, I wouldn't have let her watch it. Nonetheless, she saw it, and it was her response that brought me to full attention: "Momma, I wanted to cry."

"Excuse me? *Wanted* to cry? How can you watch an innocent man be murdered and not lose your mind?" I responded. But at the same time, I was asking myself, what lies from the world had I perpetuated in her life that kept her from fully feeling the pain from one of our own losing his life so senselessly. Then the Word of the Lord came to me: *"Why do you call me, 'Lord, Lord,' and do not do what I say?"* (Luke 6:46). *"So whoever knows the right thing to do and fails to do it, for him it is sin"* (James 4:17 ESV). What is good? *"Mankind, he has told you what is good and what it is the Lord requires of you: to act justly, to love faithfulness, and to walk humbly with your God"* (Mic. 6:8 CSB).

My fears of revealing my race dimmed compared to the pain I understood. There's a fire that has raged in my bones since that day to which I cannot put into words. All I know is that I immediately thought about Moses at a time when he was out observing his own people forced into labor. He saw an Egyptian beating a Hebrew, "one of his own people," and struck the Egyptian down before hiding him in the sand (Exod. 2:11). Moses would lose his life that day—he would no longer be a prince or know the comforts of a palace. By striking that Egyptian, he chose a side. I realized that day that I had another choice to make, and this one needed no time. Dare. *Lose your life.* All that God had been showing me finally made complete sense. How could I give God my whole heart and deny myself in the process? I could not carry on hiding my identity and say I was a follower of Christ. It just doesn't work like that. God's words rang in my ear louder than ever: *"Much will be required of everyone who has been given much. And even more will be expected of the one who has been entrusted with more"* (Luke 12:48 HCSB).

I felt so liberated. I suddenly had the most bizarre urge to stand on my roof and shout for the whole world to hear, "I am BLACK! I am BLACK! I AM BLAAACK!!!" Shackles and chains had fallen off me, and I had the strength of 10,000 men. I could've climbed the highest mountain. My house would have been a small feat:

> *What I tell you in the dark, speak in the daylight; what is whispered in your ear, proclaim from the roofs. Do not be afraid of those who kill the body but cannot kill the soul. Rather, be afraid of the One who can destroy both soul and body in hell. Are not two sparrows sold for a penny? Yet not one of them will fall to the ground*

*outside your Father's care. And even the very hairs of*
*your head are all numbered. So don't be afraid; you*
*are worth more than many sparrows.*

—Matt. 10:27–31

I was officially called that day. Silence was not an option. I had been prepped all these years for this moment. Just like Joshua had reminded the Israelites of all the places they had been where God had never left them, performed miracles, driven out their enemies, and overabundantly provided, so God took me down a familiar road, recounting all the ways He had done the same for me. At this point, it was a no-brainer: *"But if serving the LORD seems undesirable to you, then choose for yourselves this day whom you will serve"* (Josh. 24:15).

Repentance was imperative. I needed to take a few days to grieve and wrap my mind around what I had done. It was true I was a murderer. People tried to comfort me and downplay this fact, saying I was just dealt a bad hand. No. Jesus says, if you hate your brother, you are a murderer. I made a conscious decision every time I made the choice to leave my race out. It wasn't that my heart was wicked because I agreed with the injustice—I didn't agree with it at all. It was wicked because I was meant to say something, and I had been on mute my whole life. My hypocrisy was revealed. There was blood on my hands.

Just weeks before this incident, I had sat with my church in a six-week study over David Platt's *Something Needs to Change*. I agreed we should all be like the Good Samaritan—regardless of a person's status or what other people think of us, we should stand for what is right and care for the hurting. Then, as a world, we watched a man being murdered unjustly before our very eyes, and the church from where I stood was absent. Instead, people were fighting over names and statues with the notion that outward appearances were good for our hearts. Striving in our own strength amounts to nothing. I know this one. These are people's lives. For me to deny the reality of the pain plaguing our brothers and sisters at this point, would be for me to blatantly disobey and deny Him. There was not much I could do from where I sat, but I was torn up over it all.

So, I started with what I could do. Putting fear in its place, I gave my full testimony at church for the first time. In June 2020, also for the first time in my life, I asked my hairdresser not to put any blonde in my hair or straighten it. There is nothing wrong with either one of these things, and of course there is nothing wrong with appearing Hispanic, but when you intend to cover up your true identity, your intentions become wrong. I wish I could go back to the first time I straightened my hair. I was having a sleepover with one of my friends, and she suggested it. I wish I had said no. I don't want to change my hair. It's part of who I am, and I am proud of my identity. But instead, I didn't give it a second thought. I was excited to know it was even an option. I wanted nothing more than to blend in. I wanted the straight and narrow. I wanted to look "right," to act "right," to fit into the image that satisfied the way things were supposed to be as I was conditioned to believe.

The only image I want to identify with now is that of Christ. Since I have a flawed memory and easily forget God's lessons, I want my curly hair to forever be on my head to represent what my flawed humanity can't remember: a faithful God who has every hair on this head counted and purposed. I will no longer be ashamed of what He gave me. I will wear it as proudly as the brown tint on this skin. If people don't like it (and some won't), I'll just take a lesson from my momma: Smile, nod, and "bless their hearts."

# Hidden in Plain Sight

*So do not be afraid of them, for there is nothing concealed that will not be disclosed, or hidden that will not be made known.*

—Matt. 10:26

As the longest spring break in history began to finally unravel and it was time to go back to work, what I feared started to surface. Back to school. Back to "normal." I might have been the only person in America who was terrified of normal returning. I had been in such an amazing place with the Lord—all the distractions were gone, His voice was booming, and I had been made whole again. God had again done the miraculous. I knew there was no turning back this time as I vowed to follow Him, but my track record haunted me as I found myself driving down a familiar path headed back into one of my biggest places of defeat: school. Old fears began to surface and rushed over me like a wave. That 10-year-old girl started to emerge, and I did my morning ritual of crying out to the Lord and begging for him to wiggle His nose and zap me out of my dire circumstances. I began to quiet down and be still before the Lord. As I did, the Lord spoke what I believe was the mic drop to this whole experience. I heard, "Redo it." Huh? "That 10-year-old girl you wished you could go back to is about to head into another school year. Do it again. This time with Me."

I had been set free, but familiar roads had a way of triggering memories that led me straight into old mindsets. I'd run straight into the lie, taking the enemy's bait every time. Those same insecurities that developed at the age of 10 still drove my decisions. The same crowds that formed around me as a little girl were still there. They were just grown-ups. As I drove down the road the first day heading back to school, my mom's voice rang in my ear, and it made me giggle. I remembered her advice as I would complain about my drama as a teenager. She was quite the advice giver. In her country twang, she'd simply drag out, "Adults are worse." That never made me feel better, but I don't know that I'd say she was wrong. The difference was that now I understood who my real enemy was, and it was time I started living like it.

Scales fell from my eyes in a 20-minute car ride. I had been given the opportunity school year after school year, and day after day. *Do it again. This time with Me.* His mercies *were* new every morning (Lam. 3:23). This old truth I had memorized long ago now fell on me afresh. It was as if I were hearing it for the first time, and it had been there all along. It was my 39th birthday, and I felt I was receiving the greatest gift of all: freedom from the expectations of people. What I love about the Lord is that He doesn't show you your shortcomings and then leave you there. He beckons you to himself. His yoke is easy and light. He offers rest and newness. "Dang," I said to Him driving down the road, "Whitney Houston almost had it right. To love yourself is a *great* and necessary gift, but *You* are the greatest love of all. I wouldn't know love without You, Lord. Thank You, Jesus." I had been enslaved to the praise of people who said I was good enough, and I had run on the ideology that the approval of people equaled the approval of Christ. I made Jesus a white man—a white man who accepted me and chose, like myself, to ignore my Black DNA. My identity was in Christ all along, but I couldn't fully understand it because I had given Him only half of my heart. The white half. It sounds ridiculous, but if I'm being honest—I realized in that moment I had been given year after year, day after day, moment after moment to redo all the things I had undone. Each year, He put me back in a public school, He was giving me another chance to make right all I had done wrong and to face all the old hurts that the enemy constantly had on replay in my mind. They resurfaced and in that moment, God was telling me to have the courage to lean on Him right there in the face of those oppositions that defeated me day after day for decades.

*Do it again. This time with me.* I went back to school, and for an entire year, which would end up being my last, I wrestled with the King of my heart. My circumstances did not change, but I did. Instead of running out and using my old mechanisms of coping, I ran to God. I did not run out in old Kristi fashion and hide in the dark when things got too rough. It was one of the hardest times in my life and in my family's because they fought with me. In the last few weeks of my battle, I fought out in the cave I called my classroom, God would conclude the lessons He had brought to light in that place, and my story came full circle. In a book I have taught and read a thousand times, *The Watsons Go to Birmingham – 1963*, a character, Byron, is out of control in misbehavior that pushes his parents over the edge when he gets caught straightening and dying his hair. This incident causes his mom and dad to journey from their home in Michigan to their hometown of Birmingham, Alabama, in hopes of getting through to their son. They needed him to understand how dangerous it was for a young Black man during this time. Ironically, this school year was the first time my students could relate to the historical context of the narrative, but they could not understand the drastic move the boy's parents made over his hair. In light of all the other things the young boy had done, the hair incident seemed light in comparison. I agreed with them, and in my search to answer their question I found this explanation:

> During the Civil Rights movement, the conk hairstyle was particularly criticized as detrimental to the entire Black race because it involved engaging in a dangerous chemical process all for the intent of eliminating Black features in order to look more White.[3]

I understood this process all too well, but it was the next section that brought it home:

> This was particularly controversial at the time because the Black community emphasized the importance of loving one's natural self—and for many, like Momma and Dad in this story, that meant not altering your naturally curly hair.[4]

And there it was. Where it all began is where it would all end—in junior high. There was so much more to learn about these roots of mine. I am naturally curly and proud to be.

There is a great deal to say on this matter of Black and white and what it really means for an individual and the church. I have learned much about the origins of this racial conflict since God opened my eyes, and I have identified, to my amazement, with many stories from African Americans who lived decades before me. When I first read the opening lines of Maya Angelou's *I Know Why the Caged Bird Sings*, I couldn't believe what I held in my hands. My deep, dark secrets were revealed, and I realized that I had been called out by someone whom I never knew. She had the exact thoughts that I had, but I had never dared to admit them to myself or anyone else. It felt impossible that she could know. She writes:

> I was going to look like one of those sweet little white girls who was everybody's dream of what was right with the world. . . . Wouldn't they be surprised when one day I woke out of my black ugly dream, and my real hair, which was long and blond, would take the place of the kinky mass that Momma wouldn't let me straighten? My light blue eyes were going to hypnotize them. . . . Because I was really white and because a cruel fairy stepmother . . . had turned me into a too-big Negro girl, with nappy black hair.[5]

I was too awestruck with the "blonde hair and blue eyes" that I didn't even catch the meaning behind the fact that she says her mom wouldn't let her straighten it. I had always viewed Black women incredibly strong and proud of who they were with assurance that they were above any feelings of inferiority. I went on to read her experiences, and my naivety started to unravel. To say I have been clueless on understanding the history of the people I never knew, is an understatement. I never had identified with anyone in this way. We'd believed the same lie from the same age-old enemy where hate originated and from generation to generation sought to annihilate God's children. He never had anything new. We had been lured into the same vulnerabilities to the same open door meant for destruction. But God. What the enemy meant for evil, God used for good. I began to realize over time that this lack of understanding was the missing piece.

I had hidden behind the fear of my identity being known for too long as someone who claims there is only One to be feared. I was so scared that it literally took death to believe what God was telling me. In a secret part of my heart, deep down, I knew denying my identity was wrong. The tiny spark that lived in the dark recesses of my heart ignited a flame, and that tiny spark was Him all along. He is the way, the truth, and the life. Anyone who wants to find their life, must lose it in Him. He sustained me and kept my head above water all this time when I should have drowned. He saved me. I am free: *"If the Son sets you free, you shall be free indeed"* (John 8:36 ESV).

My experiences have allowed me to feel both sides of the spectrum. "White privilege" is a real thing. I know it because I've been a recipient of it. Racism against people of color is a real thing. I've been on that end, too. I didn't believe God about this for a long time. Unfortunately, He had to show me plainly.

My circumstances are rare, and not because of my upbringing with Memaw and my white, southern mom or my ability to bypass some racial inequality. My experiences are rare because of Jesus Christ. I am deeply rooted in Him and not in one political side or ethnic group. I will say, however, that I am extremely proud to admit now that I belong to both heritages. My identity is all uniquely me and I wouldn't have it any other way. It took a pure knowledge of Jesus Christ to bring me to that point. Without Him, we cannot see clearly.

There is undoubtedly tension in the church. Without exposure, we will never heal. Satan is a liar. There is no truth in him. We (the church) need to face the lies, stop acting so defensive, be honest about where we are, and collectively crush the head of the enemy. The fact that Jesus waited until the year 2020 to reveal this area of deceit in my life is astonishing to me. The length of time I've lived in this condition before Jesus said anything about it has made me realize we have a massive ability to appear so put together. We even convince ourselves that we are okay when we are not okay. Some of us are claiming the name of Jesus as Lord of our lives, but we have deep issues that keep us enslaved. *"It is for freedom that Christ has set us free. Stand firm, then, and do not let yourselves be burdened again by a yoke of slavery"* (Gal. 5:1).

Hearts are hard, and there's a lie that has existed for far too long. It has become our narrative and keeps us disillusioned and divided. It's time for the church to do what it was sent to do. Stand up against the lie, recognize it for what it is, defend the needy and seek justice.

> *Many will say to me in that day, Lord, Lord, have we not prophesied in thy name? and in thy name have cast out devils? and in thy name done many wonderful works? And then will I profess unto them, I never knew you: depart from me, ye that work iniquity.*
>
> —Matt. 7:22–23 KJV

It may be hard to receive, but it doesn't take a scholar to understand this verse. According to *Merriam-Webster's Dictionary*, the word *iniquity* means "gross injustice, wickedness; the quality of being unfair or evil." The church is on the hot seat. Those who call on the name of the Lord have a history of acting wickedly, being unfair, evil, and from what I've read in historical accounts, grossly unjust in some of the most horrendous accounts of violence and murder against God's children. Lord knows the history of the church with regard to racial injustice has been ugly, and it is not yet a thing of the past.

After that man made the racist remark against our church to my husband, it cultivated a curiosity in me that sent me on a search to find exactly what a "Black church" was and why we still have them. I knew our church wasn't Black because we had red brick and white siding. I also knew he wasn't referring to its exterior color. After many sleepless nights, I found an explanation to my questions, and it was not hard to understand the role that slavery played in the development of separate worship services for whites and Blacks. According to what we are experiencing today, I could also see why we still had separate worship services but based on the Word of God, this should not be so. Jesus prayed for unity for all believers. It's the condition of our hearts that is at stake, not which church we attend. Hear the Word of the Lord: *"Your incense is detestable to Me. New Moons and Sabbaths, and the calling of solemn assemblies—I cannot stand iniquity with a festival"* (Isa. 1:13 HCSB). There's that word again, *iniquity*. He hates that.

It's a burden to Him for us to come back week after week in the same condition. Even if we offer countless prayers, He won't listen. *"Your hands are covered with blood,"* He says in Isaiah 1:15 (HCSB). In other words, your worship stinks, literally. He says it has a "stench," and He wants no part in it (Amos 5:21). If we operate with iniquity in our hearts, detected or not, we worship in error. God is disgusted by this.

There are false prophets among us. They are really good liars who are easy to follow, but God says, we will know them by their fruit. There are many, an indefinite number of people—many,

many, many—who will follow. Jesus said if you hate your brother, you are a murderer. If you are a murderer, you have blood on your hands. Murder begins in the heart. First John 3:14–15 (HCSB) tells us:

> We know that we have passed from death to life because we love our brothers. The one who does not love remains in death. Everyone who hates his brother is a murderer, and you know that no murderer has eternal life residing in him.

But there is hope.

People are dying right now at a rate unusual to me. Many are facing our Lord Jesus Christ at this very hour. It is not God's desire that anyone should perish, but there will come a time when there is no more time. The day I realized how sick my heart was, I could have argued I was just a step away from being one of the "many" who had been invited but didn't quite make the cut. I spent days in anguish. I realized as Isaiah did, "Woe to me! . . . For I am a man of unclean lips" (Isa. 6:5). But what did God do afterward? He took the coal, touched Isaiah's lips, atoned for his sins, and took his guilt away. There is nothing we can do but receive it. "The Lord does not delay His promise, as some understand delay, but is patient with you, not wanting any to perish but all to come to repentance" (2 Pet. 3:9 HCSB).

So, clothe yourselves in righteousness:

> Put to death, therefore, whatever belongs to your earthly nature: sexual immorality, impurity, lust, evil desires and greed, which is idolatry. Because of these, the wrath of God is coming. You used to walk in these

*ways, in the life you once lived. But now you must also rid yourselves of all such things as these: anger, rage, malice, slander, and filthy language from your lips. Do not lie to each other, since you have taken off your old self with its practices and have put on the new self, which is being renewed in knowledge in the image of its Creator. Here there is no Gentile or Jew, circumcised or uncircumcised, barbarian, Scythian, slave or free, but Christ is all, and is in all. Therefore, as God's chosen people, holy and dearly loved, clothe yourselves with compassion, kindness, humility, gentleness and patience. Bear with each other and forgive one another if any of you has a grievance against someone. Forgive as the LORD forgave you. And over all these virtues put on love, which binds them all together in perfect unity.*

—Col. 3:5–14

He rights every wrong. He leaves no stone unturned. He is so attentive to every need and whim if we will let Him be. Let Him. God is a redeemer. He ties up all the loose ends, and He loves us deeply. He is the One who will break through the toughest of hearts and cut straight to what really matters. There are no extraneous details with the Lord. Every word He speaks matters, and everything has significance.

God's love for us is far beyond our comprehension. He laid down His life for His sheep. False prophets are running rampant, and it is therefore imperative to know your Shepherd's voice so that you follow only Him. Clear your conscience before the Lord. I will present the same question that was presented to me not long after I came to the true realization of my condition: *"How long will you . . . pursue a lie?"* (Ps. 4:2 HCSB). When we are presented with the truth, we are held accountable for what we choose to do with it. We can't hide. Pour over the scriptures. Learn and fall in love with Him. Know Him. Talk to Him. He hears you. He sees you. He still speaks, and I promise you, He can't wait to welcome you back home.

# 10-Year-Old Me

*Be strong and courageous; don't be terrified or afraid of them. For it is the LORD your God who goes with you; He will not leave you or forsake you.*

*—Deuteronomy 31:6 HCSB*

My walk with the Lord began the moment I stepped out onto the red carpet of that tiny Baptist church in 1989. My experience was authentic, but I'd heard only half the story. If I could go back to that 10-year-old girl who was left alone and thrown to the wolves, I would. I'd walk with her and explain what had just happened. I would tell her that she was a sheep called by her Shepherd into the sheepfold. But sheep have enemies who sneak in, and there are wolves who attack where the Shepherd has placed the sheep to have good pasture. I would say to the 10-year-old me:

> The enemy comes to steal, kill, and destroy. Do not worry, however, because the Lord is your Shepherd. He stands at the gate and will not allow anything to get to

you that does not pass through His hands first. He will protect you and be with you every step of the way. He will always send you what you need, but you have to accept it. Life may not look the way you think it should. Trust Him. He knows what's best for you. Keep going to church and talking to your leaders about what's going on. Don't be ashamed. You'll be surprised how many people deal with the same struggles.

You are biracial, which means you are a part of two different races. Neither is better than the other. You have rock star parents who know what's right and aren't swayed by people's opinions. You don't have to pick a side no matter what people may tell you. You are fearfully and wonderfully made. The world has a warped mind over this, and you may have a lot of enemies right now. The good news is this: You are not of this world. You are God's, and your true identity is in Him. It's going to be hard, but it won't always be this way. Don't let the world label you. Believe what God says about you because in reality, you're not "Black" or "white." You were made in God's image, created for good works, which He prepared beforehand that you should walk in them (Eph. 2:10).

Do not be conformed to this world. Your hair is your crown. Wear it proudly. You can straighten your hair if *you* want to, but don't do so to cover up any part of who you are, and don't let any roots of bitterness be your guide. Love your enemies and pray for them. You're safe in the arms of Jesus. I promise. He will never leave you or forsake you, even when you get older. You're going to mess up. He knows. Repent, believe, and act on what you believe.

# Notes

1. Wikipedia, s.v. "Dixie," December 2020, https://en.wikipedia .org/wiki/Dixie.
2. Priscilla Shirer, *Fervent: A Woman's Battle Plan to Serious, Specific, and Strategic Prayer* (Nashville, TN: B&H Publishing Group, 2015), 99.
3. An Educator's Resource for "The Watson's Go to Birmingham," https://www.walden.com/wp-content/uploads/2013/06/The -Watsons-go-to-Birmingham-Educational-Resource.pdf.
4. Ibid.
5. Maya Angelou, *I Know Why the Caged Bird Sings* (New York: Ballantine Books, 2015), 2–3.

# About the Author

**Kristi Sanders Lasher** was born in Dallas, Texas, as a biracial child in the 1980s. Kristi's cherished childhood created a deep love for her southern roots, yet a racially divided culture made her deeply afraid of revealing her true identity. Kristi tried to hide her ethnicity well into adulthood until God captivated her, uncovered her secret, and set her free. Kristi serves alongside her husband in pastoring a small Baptist church in Gause, Texas, as they raise their three beautiful teenage children. Kristi was a public school teacher for many years, and she holds a master's degree in worship leadership studies from Dallas Baptist University.